Fish of Minnesota

FIELD GUIDE · 2ND EDITION

T0162985

by Dave Bosanko

Adventure Publications
Cambridge, Minnesota

ACKNOWLEDGMENTS

Special thanks to Dave Bierman from the Iowa Department of Natural Resources for reviewing this book. Thanks also to the United States Fish and Wildlife Service and the Minnesota Department of Natural Resources.

Edited by Brett Ortler

Cover and book design by Jonathan Norberg

Illustration credits by artist and page number:
Cover Illustrations: Channel Catfish (main) and Bluegill (upper front and back cover) by **Duane Raver/USFWS**

Timothy Knepp/USFWS: 90 (both), 92, 104 (main), 106; **MyFWC.com/fishing:** 13; **Duane Raver/USFWS:** 11, 19, 22, 24, 26, 28, 30, 32, 34, 36, 42, 44, 46, 48, 52, 62, 72 (second inset), 78, 86, 88, 94, 96 (top), 100, 124, 126, 128, 138, 140, 142, 144, 146, 148, 150, 152, 156, 158, 162;
Joseph Tomelleri: 10, 38 (both), 40, 50, 54, 56 (both), 58, 60, 64, 66 (both), 68, 70 (both), 72 (both), 74, 76, 80 (both), 82, 84 (both), 96 (bottom), 98 (all), 102, 108, 110, 112, 114, 116, 118 (both), 120, 122, 130, 132, 134, 136, 154, 160, 164.

10 9 8 7 6 5 4

Fish of Minnesota Field Guide
First Edition 2007
Second Edition 2019
Copyright © 2007 and 2019 by David Bosanko
Published by Adventure Publications
An imprint of AdventureKEEN
310 Garfield Street South
Cambridge, Minnesota 55008
(800) 678-7006
www.adventurepublications.net
Printed in China
ISBN 978-1-59193-790-6 (pbk.); ISBN 978-1-59193-791-3 (ebook)

TABLE OF CONTENTS

Trout-Perch Family

WHAT'S NEW IN THE SECOND EDITION

First released in 2007, *Fish of Minnesota* has made fish identification easy for more than a decade. Now including 81 species, this revised and expanded second edition offers even more. Here's what's new in the second edition:

More Species: Six additional fish species are included in this book; several are aquatic invasive species, so it's especially important to be on the lookout for them. The new additions are the Silver Carp, the Bighead Carp, the White Perch, the Blue Catfish, the Round Goby, and the Ruffe.

Fishing Tips: Popular game species now feature fishing tips to help you land that lunker.

Revised and Updated: Whether it's a new state fishing record, the advance of invasive species, or updated range information, each account has been carefully reviewed and updated to reflect the latest developments in the angling world and fisheries science.

The Same Stuff You Know and Love: As always, the book features world-class illustrations, fascinating facts about each species' range, natural history, and more.

HOW TO USE THIS BOOK

The fish are organized by family, such as Catfish (Ictaluridae), Perch (Percidae) and Sunfish (Centrarchidae). Each family is then listed in alphabetical order. Within these families, individual species are arranged alphabetically by common name in their appropriate groups. For example, members of the Sunfish family are divided into the Black

Bass, Crappie, and True Sunfish groups. For a detailed list of fish families and individual species, turn to the Table of Contents (pg. 3); the Index (pg. 172) provides a reference guide to fish by common name (such as Mooneye) and other common terms for the species.

Fish Identification

Determining a fish's body shape is the first step to identifying it. Each fish family usually exhibits one or sometimes two basic outlines. Catfish have long, stout bodies with flattened heads; barbels or "whiskers" around the mouth; a relatively tall, but narrow, dorsal fin; and an adipose fin. There are two forms of Sunfish: the flat, round, plate-like outline we see in Bluegills, and the torpedo or "fusiform" shape of Largemouth Bass.

In this field guide, you can quickly identify a fish by first matching its general body shape to one of the fish family silhouettes listed in the Table of Contents (pg. 3). From there, turn to that family's section, and use the illustrations and text descriptions to identify your fish. Sample Pages (pg. 22) are provided to explain how the information is presented in each two-page spread.

For some species, the illustration will be enough to identify your catch, but it is important to note that your fish may not look exactly like the artwork. Fish frequently change colors. Males that are brightly colored during the spawning season may show muted coloration at other times. Likewise, bass caught in muddy streams show much less pattern than those taken from clear lakes—and all fish lose some of their markings and color when removed from the water.

Most fish are similar in appearance to one or more other species—often, but not always, within the same family. For example, the Walleye is remarkably similar to the Sauger. To accurately identify such look-alikes, check the inset illustrations and accompanying notes below the main illustration, under the "Similar Species" heading.

Throughout *Fish of Minnesota* we use basic biological and fisheries management terms that refer to physical characteristics or conditions of fish and their environment, such as "dorsal fin" or "turbid water." For your convenience, these are listed and defined in the Glossary (pg. 166).

Understanding such terminology will help you make sense of reports on state and federal research, fish population surveys, lake assessments, management plans, and other important fisheries documents.

FISH ANATOMY

To identify fish, you will need to know a few basic terms that apply to fins and their locations.

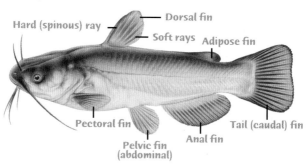

Hard (spinous) ray — Dorsal fin — Soft rays — Adipose fin

Pectoral fin — Pelvic fin (abdominal) — Anal fin — Tail (caudal) fin

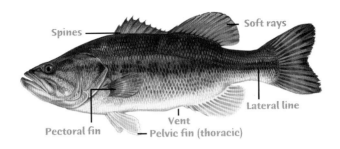

Fins are made up of bony structures that support a membrane. There are three kinds of bony structures in fins. **Soft rays** are flexible fin supports that are sometimes branched. **Spines** are stiff, often sharp, supports that are not jointed. **Hard rays** are stiff, pointed, barbed structures that can be raised or lowered. Catfish are famous for their hard rays, which are mistakenly called spines. Sunfish have soft rays associated with spines to form a dorsal fin.

Fins are named by their position on the fish. The **dorsal fin** is on the top along the midline. A few fish have another fin on their back called an **adipose fin**. This is a small, fleshy protuberance located between the dorsal fin and the tail and is distinctive of trout and catfish.

On each side of the fish near the gills are the **pectoral fins**. The **anal fin** is located along the midline on the fish's bottom or ventral side. There is also a paired set of fins on the bottom of the fish called the **pelvic fins**. Pelvic fins can be in the **thoracic position** just below the pectoral fins or farther back on the stomach in the **abdominal position**. The tail is known as the **caudal fin**.

Eyes—In general, fish have good eyesight. They can see color, but the light level they require to see well varies by species. For example, Walleyes see well in low light, whereas Bluegills have excellent daytime vision but see poorly at night, making them vulnerable to predation. Catfish have poor vision both night and day.

Nostrils—A pair of nostrils, or nares, is used to detect odors in the water. Eels and catfish have particularly well-developed senses of smell.

Mouth—The shape of the mouth is a clue to what the fish eats. The larger the food it consumes, the larger the mouth.

Teeth—Not all fish have teeth, but those that do have teeth use them to feed. Walleyes, northern pike, and muskies have sharp canine teeth for grabbing and holding prey. Minnows have teeth—located in the throat and used for grinding. Catfish have cardiform teeth, which feel like a rough patch in the front of the mouth. Bass have tiny patches of vomerine teeth in the roof of the mouth.

Swim Bladder—Almost all fish have a swim bladder, a balloon-like organ that helps the fish regulate its buoyancy.

Lateral Line—This sensory organ helps the fish detect movement in the water (to help avoid predators or capture prey) as well as water currents and pressure changes. It consists of fluid-filled sacs with hair-like sensors, which are open to the water through a row of pores in the skin along each side. These pores create a visible line down the middle of the fish's side.

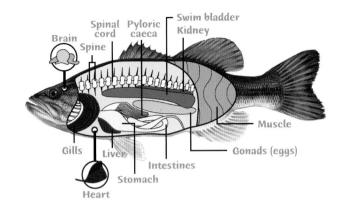

FISH NAMES

A Walleye is a Walleye in Minnesota, where it reigns as king of the game fish. But in the northern part of its range, Canadians call it a jack or jackfish. In the eastern United States, it is often grouped with pike-shaped fish and called a walleyed pickerel or walleyed pike.

Because common names may vary regionally, and even change for different sizes of the same species, scientific names are used, and they are exactly the same around the world. Each species has only one correct scientific name that can be recognized anywhere, in any language. The Walleye is *Sander vitreus* from Minneapolis to Moscow.

Scientific names are made up of Greek or Latin words that often describe the species. There are two parts to a scientific name: the generic or "genus," which is capitalized (*Sander*), and the specific name, which is not capitalized (*vitreus*). Both are displayed in italic text or underlined.

A species' genus represents a group of closely related fish. The Walleye and Sauger are in the same genus, so they share the generic name *Sander*. But each fish has a different specific name, *vitreus* for Walleye, *canadensis* for Sauger.

ABOUT MINNESOTA FISH

There are about 12,000 permanent bodies of water in Minnesota and 18,000 miles of fishable streams and rivers, adding up to 7,300 square miles of water surface. Add to this the 2,546 square miles representing Minnesota's portion of Lake Superior, and more than 8 percent of the state is covered with water.

This abundance of fresh water provides nearly a limitless number of fish habitats. It is now believed that there are about 165 species of fish inhabiting Minnesota waters, 30 of which are targeted by recreational anglers. About another 40 to 50 species are of particular interest to those that spend time near the water because of their status as bait, their unique characteristics, or the likelihood that you will see them on forays to various freshwater habitats.

The fish species included in this book cover Minnesota's sport fish and representatives of all the common fish families found in Minnesota.

FREQUENTLY ASKED QUESTIONS

What is a fish?

Fish are aquatic, typically cold-blooded animals that have backbones, gills, and fins.

Are all fish cold-blooded?

All freshwater fish are cold-blooded. Recently, it has been discovered that a few saltwater fish, including some members of the Tuna family, are warm-blooded. Whales and Bottlenose Dolphins are also warm-blooded, but they are mammals, not fish.

Do all fish have scales?

No. Most fish have scales that look like those on the Common Goldfish. A few, such as Alligator Gar, have scales that resemble armor plates. Catfish have no scales at all.

How do fish breathe?

A fish takes in water through its mouth and forces it through its gills, where a system of fine membranes absorbs oxygen from the water and releases carbon dioxide. Gills cannot pump air efficiently over these membranes, which quickly dry out and stick together. Fish should never be out of the water longer than you can hold your breath.

Can fish breathe air?

Some species can; gar have a modified swim bladder that acts like a lung. Fish that can't breathe air may die when dissolved oxygen in the water falls below critical levels.

How do fish swim?

Fish swim by contracting bands of muscles on alternate sides of their body so the tail is whipped rapidly from side to side. Pectoral and pelvic fins are used mainly for stability when a fish hovers but are sometimes used during rapid bursts of forward motion.

Do all fish look like fish?

Most do and are easily recognizable as fish. The eels and lampreys are fish, but they look like snakes. Sculpins look like little goblins with bat wings.

Where can you find fish?

Some fish species can be found in almost any body of water, but not all fish are found everywhere. Each species has adapted to exploit a particular habitat. A species may move around within its home water, sometimes migrating hundreds of miles between lakes, rivers, and tributary streams. Some movements, such as spawning migrations, are seasonal and very predictable.

Fish may also move horizontally from one area to another, or vertically in the water column, in response to changes in environmental conditions and food availability. In addition, many fish have daily travel patterns. By studying a species' habitat, food, and spawning information in this book— and understanding how it interacts with other Minnesota fish—it is possible to make an educated prediction of where to find it in any lake, stream, or river.

FISH DISEASES

Fish are susceptible to various parasites, infections, and diseases. Some diseases have little effect on fish populations, while others may have a devastating impact. While fish diseases can't be transmitted to humans, they may render the fish inedible. To prevent the spread of such diseases, don't transfer any fish from one body of water to another. Information on Minnesota fish diseases can be

found at the DNR website www.dnr.state.mn.us
/fish_diseases/index.html.

INVASIVE SPECIES

While some introduced species have great recreational
value (Rainbow Trout, for example), many exotic species
have caused problems. Helping limit the spread of these
nuisance species is everyone's responsibility. Never move
fish, water, or vegetation from one lake or stream
to another, and always follow state recommendations
on protecting our state's waters. Details about aquatic
invasive species are available at the Minnesota DNR
website: www.dnr.state.mn.us/invasives/ais/index.html

FUN WITH FISH

There are many ways to enjoy Minnesota's fish, from read-
ing about them in this book to watching them in the wild.
Hands-on activities are also popular. Many resident and
nonresident anglers enjoy pursuing Minnesota's game fish.
The sport offers a great chance to enjoy the outdoors with
friends and family and, in many cases, bring home a healthy
meal of fresh fish.

Proceeds from license sales, along with special taxes anglers
pay on fishing supplies and motorboat fuel, fund the major-
ity of fish management efforts, including fish surveys, the
development of special regulations, and stocking programs.
The sport also has a huge impact on Minnesota's economy,
supporting thousands of jobs in fishing, tourism, and
related industries.

CATCH-AND-RELEASE FISHING

Selective harvest (keeping some fish to eat and releasing the rest) and total catch-and-release fishing allow anglers to enjoy the sport without harming the resource. Catch-and-release is especially important with certain species and sizes of fish, and in lakes or rivers where biologists are trying to improve the fishery by protecting adult fish of breeding age. Many lakes now have mandatory slot limits requiring anglers to release fish of a certain length. Before you head out, check the DNR's website for slot limits on the lakes you'll be fishing: www.dnr.state.mn.us/regulations/fishing/index.html

Catch-and-release is only truly successful if the fish survives the experience. Here are some helpful tips to reduce the chances of post-release mortality:

- Play and land fish quickly.
- Wet your hands before touching a fish to avoid removing its protective slime coating.
- Handle the fish gently and keep it in the water as much as possible.
- Do not hold the fish by the eyes or gills. Hold it by the lower lip or under the gill plate—and support its belly.
- If a fish is deeply hooked, cut the line so at least an inch hangs outside the mouth. This helps the hook lie flat when the fish takes in food.
- Circle hooks may help reduce the number of deeply hooked fish.
- Avoid fishing in deep water unless you plan to keep your catch.

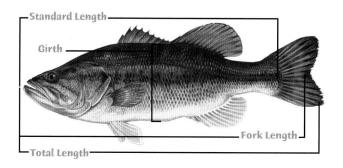

FISH MEASUREMENT

The are three ways to measure fish: standard length (from the tip of the snout to just before the tail), fork length (from the tip of the snout to the middle of the tail fork), and total length. The first two are more accurate because tails are often damaged. In Minnesota, total length is used in slot limits; it's also what anglers commonly measure. To measure a fish's total length, pinch the tail together to make the fish as long as possible. The following formulas estimate the weight of popular fish. The total length is in inches; weight is in pounds.

Formulas

Bass weight = (length x length x girth) / 1,200
Pike weight = (length x length x length) / 3,500
Sunfish weight = (length x length x length) / 1,200
Trout weight = (length x girth x girth) / 800
Walleye weight = (length x length x length) / 2,700

Let's say that you catch a 16-inch Walleye. Using the formula for Walleyes above: (16 x 16 x 16) divided by 2,700 = 1.5 pounds. Your Walleye would weigh approximately 1.5 pounds.

MINNESOTA STATE RECORD FISH

SPECIES	WEIGHT (LB.-OZ.)	LENGTH (IN.)	WHERE CAUGHT	YEAR
Bass, Largemouth	8-15	23.5	Auburn Lake	2005
Bass, Rock	2-0	13.5	Lake Osakis	1998
Bass, Smallmouth	8-0	N/A	W. Battle Lake	1948
Bass, White	4-8	20	Vadnais Lake	2016
Bowfin	12-9	31.5	Mississippi River	2012
Buffalo, Bigmouth	41-11	38.5	Mississippi River	1991
Buffalo, Black	20-0.5	34.2	Minnesota River	1997
Buffalo, Smallmouth	20-0	32	Big Sandy Lake	2003
Bullhead, Black	3-12	17.17	Reno Lake	1997
Bullhead, Brown	7-1	24.4	Shallow Lake	1974
Bullhead, Yellow	3-10.5	17.9	Lake Osakis	2002
Burbot	19-10	33	Lake of the Woods	2016
Carp, Common	55-5	42	Clearwater Lake	1952
Carpsucker, River	4-6	21.6	Minnesota River	2012
Catfish, Blue	52-8	48	Minnesota River	2002
Catfish, Channel	38-0	44	Mississippi	1975
Catfish, Flathead	70-0	N/A	St. Croix River	1970
Crappie, Black	5-0	21	Vermillion River	1940
Crappie, White	3-15	18	Lake Constance	2002
Drum, Freshwater	35-3	36	Mississippi River	1999
Eel, American	6-9	42	St. Croix River	1997
Gar, Longnose	16-12	53	St. Croix River	1982
Gar, Shortnose	5-4	31	Minnesota River	2017
Goldeye	2-13.1	20.1	Root River	2001
Hogsucker, Northern	1-15	14.25	Sunrise River	1982
Mooneye	1-15	16.5	Minnesota River	1980
Muskellunge	54-0	56	Lake Winnibigoshish	1957
Muskellunge, Tiger	34-12	51	Lake Elmo	1999
Northern, Pike	45-12	N/A	Basswood Lake	1929
Perch, Yellow	3-4	N/A	Lake Plantagenet	1945
Quillback	6-14.4	23	Mississippi River	1991
Redhorse, Golden	4-7	21	Root River	2017
Redhorse, Greater	12-11.5	28.5	Sauk River	2005
Redhorse, River	12-10	28.38	Kettle River	2005
Redhorse, Shorthead	7-15	27	Rum River	1983
Redhorse, Silver	10-6	26.75	Rainy River	2018
Salmon, Atlantic	12-13	35.5	Baptism River	1991

SPECIES	WEIGHT (LB.-OZ.)	LENGTH (IN.)	WHERE CAUGHT	YEAR
Salmon, Chinook	33-4	44.75	Poplar River	1989
Salmon, Coho	10-6.5	27.3	Lake Superior	1970
Salmon, Kokanee	2-15	20	Caribou Lake	1971
Salmon, Pink	4-8	23.5	Cascade River	1989
Sauger	6-2.2	23.9	Mississippi River	1988
Saugeye	9-13.4	27	Mississippi River	1999
Splake	13-5.44	33.5	Larson Lake	2001
Sturgeon, Lake	94-4	70	Kettle River	1994
Sturgeon, Shovelnose	6-7	33	Mississippi River	2012
Sucker, Blue	14-3	30.4	Mississippi River	1987
Sucker, Longnose	3-10.6	21	Brule River	2005
Sucker, White	9-1	24.5	Big Fish Lake	1983
Sunfish, Bluegill	2-13	N/A	Alice Lake	1948
Sunfish, Green	1-4.8	10.25	North Arbor Lake	2005
Sunfish, Hybrid	1-12	11.5	Zumbro River	1994
Sunfish, Pumpkinseed	1-5.6	10.1	Leech Lake	1999
Trout, Brook	6-5.6	24	Pigeon River	2000
Trout, Brown	16-12	31.4	Lake Superior	1989
Trout, Lake	43-8	N/A	Lake Superior	1955
Trout, Rainbow	16-6	33	Devil Track River	1980
Trout, Tiger	2-9.12	20	Mill Creek	1999
Tullibee (Cisco)	5-11.8	20.45	Little Long Lake	2002
Walleye	17-8	35.8	Seagull River	1979
Whitefish, Lake	12-4.5	28.5	Leech Lake	1999
Whitefish, Round	2-7.5	21	Lake Superior	1987

FISH CONSUMPTION ADVISORIES

Most fish are safe to eat, but pollutants are a valid concern. Minnesota routinely monitors contaminant levels and issues advisories and recommendations about eating sport fish caught in the wild. For up-to-date fish consumption guidelines where you're fishing in Minnesota, visit: Minnesota Department of Health: www.health.state.mn.us /divs/eh/fish/

These pages explain how the information is presented for each fish.

SAMPLE FISH ILLUSTRATION

Description: brief summary of physical characteristics to help you identify the fish, such as coloration and markings, body shape, fin size, and placement

Similar Species: lists other fish that look similar and the pages on which they can be found; also includes detailed inset drawings (below) highlighting physical traits such as markings, mouth size or shape, and fin characteristics to help you distinguish this fish from similar species

Walleye	Sauger	Saugeye
spiny dorsal with indistinct spots, dark blotch on rear base	spiny dorsal with distinct spots, no blotch on rear base	spiny dorsal with distinct spots, dark blotch on rear base

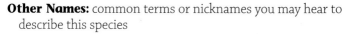

COMMON NAME
Scientific Name

Other Names: common terms or nicknames you may hear to describe this species

Habitat: environment where the fish is found (such as streams, rivers, small or large lakes, fast-flowing or still water, in or around vegetation, near shore, in clear water)

Range: geographic distribution, starting with the fish's overall range, followed by state-specific information

Food: what the fish eats most of the time (such as crustaceans, insects, fish, plankton)

Reproduction: timing of and behavior during the spawning period (dates and water temperatures, migration information, preferred spawning habitat, type of nest if applicable, colonial or solitary nester, parental care for eggs or fry)

Record and Average Size: Minnesota state record if applicable, see pg. 20 for a listing of Minnesota state records; the average size of fish caught in Minnesota

Fishing ⬤ Tip: Tips to help you catch more fish.

Notes: Interesting natural history information. This can include unique behaviors; remarkable features; sporting and table quality; details on migrations, seasonal patterns; or population trends.

Description: brownish-green back and sides with a white belly; long, stout body; rounded tail; continuous dorsal fin; bony plates covering head; males have a large "eye" spot at the base of the tail

Similar Species: Burbot (pg. 40)

Bowfin	**Burbot**	**Bowfin**	**Burbot**

no barbel on chin	small barbel on chin	one dorsal fin, short anal fin	two dorsals, long anal fin

BOWFIN
Amia calva

Other Names: dogfish, grindle or grinnel, mudfish, cypress trout, lake lawyer, beaverfish

Habitat: deep water associated with vegetation in warmwater lakes and rivers; feeds in shallow weedbeds

Range: the Mississippi River drainage east through the St. Lawrence drainage, south from Texas to Florida; Minnesota—central and southern Minnesota; not found in the drainages of the Hudson Bay or Lake Superior

Food: fish, crayfish

Reproduction: in spring when water exceeds 61 degrees, male removes vegetation to build a 2-foot-wide nest in sand or gravel; one or more females deposit up to 5,000 eggs in nest; male tenaciously guards the nest and "ball" of young

Record and Average Size: Minnesota state record—12 lb., 9 oz., 31.5 in.; Average size—2 to 5 lb. and 12 to 24 in.

Fishing ⬤Tip: Cast large, active plugs along weedbeds close to deep water at night.

Notes: A voracious predator, the Bowfin prowls shallow weedbeds, preying on anything that moves. Once thought detrimental to game fish populations, it is now considered an asset in controlling rough fish and stunted game fish. An air breather that tolerates low oxygen levels, the Bowfin can survive short periods buried in mud.

Description: black to olive-green back; sides yellowish green; belly creamy white to yellow; light bar at base of tail; barbels around mouth are dark at base; adipose fin; lacks scales; round tail; anal fin 17 to 21 rays

Similar Species: Brown Bullhead (pg. 28), Yellow Bullhead (pg. 30), Flathead Catfish (pg. 36), Madtom/Stonecat (pg. 38)

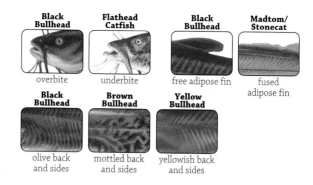

Black Bullhead	**Flathead Catfish**	**Black Bullhead**	**Madtom/ Stonecat**
overbite	underbite	free adipose fin	fused adipose fin

Black Bullhead	**Brown Bullhead**	**Yellow Bullhead**
olive back and sides	mottled back and sides	yellowish back and sides

BLACK BULLHEAD

Ameiurus melas

Other Names: common bullhead, horned pout

Habitat: shallow, slow-moving streams and backwaters; lakes and ponds; tolerates extremely turbid conditions

Range: Southern Canada through the Great Lakes and the Mississippi River watershed into the Southwest and Mexico; Minnesota—statewide

Food: a scavenging opportunist; animal material (dead or alive), some plant matter

Reproduction: spawns from late April to early June; builds nest in shallow water with a muddy bottom; both sexes guard nest, eggs, and young (until they are 1-inch long)

Record and Average Size: Minnesota Record—3 lb., 13 oz., 17.17 in.; Average Size—4 to 16 oz. and 8 to 10 in.

Fishing ◯ Tip: In still water, fish the bottom with worms or cut bait.

Notes: The smallest and most abundant of the three bullhead species, it is also the most tolerant of silt, pollution, and low oxygen levels. The number of Black Bullheads has greatly increased since the 1920s. Bullheads get little respect from most anglers, but they are tasty and often larger than most of the panfish taken home to eat.

Description: yellowish brown upper body, with mottling on back and sides; barbels around mouth; adipose fin; scaleless body; rounded tail; well-defined barbs on the pectoral spines: anal fin 22 to 23 rays

Similar Species: Black Bullhead (pg. 26), Yellow Bullhead (pg. 30), Flathead Catfish (pg. 36), Madtom/Stonecat (pg. 38)

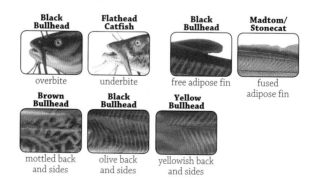

Black Bullhead	**Flathead Catfish**	**Black Bullhead**	**Madtom/ Stonecat**
overbite	underbite	free adipose fin	fused adipose fin

Brown Bullhead	**Black Bullhead**	**Yellow Bullhead**
mottled back and sides	olive back and sides	yellowish back and sides

BROWN BULLHEAD

Ameiurus nebulosus

Other Names: marbled or speckled bullhead, red cat

Habitat: warm, weedy lakes and sluggish streams

Range: Southern Canada through the Great Lakes down to the East Coast to Florida; introduced in the West; Minnesota—common in southern Minnesota; less common in the north, and absent from the Lake Superior drainage

Food: a scavenging opportunist; feeds mostly on insects, fish, fish eggs, snails, and leeches but will eat plant matter

Reproduction: in early summer male builds nest in shallow water with good vegetation and a sandy or rocky bottom; both sexes guard the eggs and young

Record and Average Size: Minnesota Record—7 lb., 1 oz., 24.4 in.; Average Size—8 oz. to 2 lb. and 8 to 12 in.

Fishing ⬤ Tip: At night, still fish on the bottom with worms or cut bait. The meat is red, firm, and very good when pan-fried.

Notes: The Brown Bullhead is very abundant in Mississippi River backwaters, but it also inhabits northern lakes. They can tolerate very turbid conditions but prefer clean water with weedy cover and a soft bottom. Adults are very involved in rearing their young, first by agitating the eggs to incubate them, then guarding the fry until they grow to about 1 inch long. The young are black and can often be seen swimming in a tight, swarming ball.

Description: olive head and back; yellowish-green sides; white belly; barbels on lower jaw are pale green or white; adipose fin; scaleless body; rounded tail; anal fin 24 to 27 rays

Similar Species: Black Bullhead (pg. 26), Brown Bullhead (pg. 28), Flathead Catfish (pg. 36), Madtom/Stonecat (pg. 38)

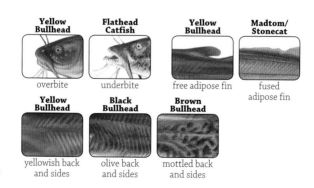

Yellow Bullhead
overbite

Flathead Catfish
underbite

Yellow Bullhead
free adipose fin

Madtom/ Stonecat
fused adipose fin

Yellow Bullhead
yellowish back and sides

Black Bullhead
olive back and sides

Brown Bullhead
mottled back and sides

YELLOW BULLHEAD

Ameiurus natalis

Other Names: white-whiskered bullhead, yellow cat

Habitat: well-vegetated, warm lakes and sluggish streams

Range: Southern Great Lakes through the eastern half of the U.S. to the Gulf and into Mexico; introduced in the west; Minnesota—lower two-thirds of the state

Food: a scavenging opportunist, feeds on insects, crayfish, snails, small fish, and plant material

Reproduction: in late spring to early summer, males build nests in shallow water with some vegetation and a soft bottom; both sexes guard the eggs and young

Record and Average Size: Minnesota state record—3 lb., 10.5 oz., 17.87 in.; Average Size—½ to 1½ lb. and 8 to 10 in.

Fishing ⬤ Tip: Still fish the lake bottom with worms or cut bait.

Notes: The Yellow Bullhead is the bullhead species least tolerant of turbidity, and it prefers low-gradient streams but will occupy reasonably clear lakes. Bullheads feed by "taste," locating food by following chemical trails through the water. This ability can be greatly diminished in polluted water, impairing their ability to find food. The Yellow Bullhead is less likely than other bullhead species to overpopulate a lake and become stunted.

Description: pale blue back and sides, large fish may be dark bluish-gray; no spots; forked tail; anal fin straight on rear edge with 30 to 35 rays; adipose fin; lacks scales; long barbels around a small mouth

Similar Species: Channel Catfish (pg. 34), Flathead Catfish (pg. 36), Bullheads (pp. 26–30)

Blue Catfish

deeply forked tail

Flathead Catfish

squared tail

Bullheads

tail rounded or slightly notched

Blue Catfish

anal fin straight, with 30 or more rays

Channel Catfish

anal fin curved, with 24 to 29 rays

BLUE CATFISH
Ictalurus furcatus

Other Names: white, silver, Mississippi or river cat

Habitat: swift current or deep, flowing pools in large rivers and impoundments; stocked in smaller impoundments for specialized fishing

Range: the Mississippi and Ohio River drainages in the central U.S.; introduced in the West; Minnesota— the lower Mississippi and Minnesota Rivers

Food: small fish; often dead or injured shad

Reproduction: adults mature at 4 to 6 years; spawning occurs in sheltered areas at the edge of currents, often in cavities or behind rocks; eggs and fry are guarded by adults

Record and Average Size: Minnesota state record—52 lb., 8 oz., 48 in.; Average Size—15 to 25 lb. and 1 to 2 feet

Fishing Tip: Fish in deep moving water with a ledge, such as the edge of a shipping channel.

Notes: The Blue Catfish is a rare fish in Minnesota. They are big fish that inhabit the fast waters of large rivers. Before many Midwestern rivers were dammed, they were once widespread here, but they now are very uncommon. Limited stocking has been unsuccessful. Blue Catfish are often mistaken for older Channel Catfish, so be sure to check the mouth and count the anal fins to identify your catch.

Description: steel gray to silver on the back and sides; white belly; young fish have black spots on the sides; large fish lack spots and appear dark olive or slate gray; forked tail; adipose fin; long barbels around mouth; anal fin with rounded edge

Similar Species: Blue Catfish (pg. 32), Flathead Catfish (pg. 36), Bullheads (pp. 26–30)

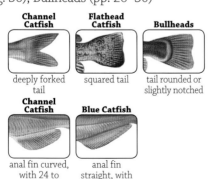

Channel Catfish
deeply forked tail

Flathead Catfish
squared tail

Bullheads
tail rounded or slightly notched

Channel Catfish
anal fin curved, with 24 to 29 rays

Blue Catfish
anal fin straight, with 30 or more rays

CHANNEL CATFISH
Ictalurus punctatus

Other Names: spotted, speckled, or silver catfish

Habitat: prefers clean, fast-moving streams with deep pools; stocked in many lakes; can tolerate turbid waters

Range: Southern Canada through the Midwest to the Gulf of Mexico into Mexico and Florida; introduced in most states; Minnesota—Mississippi and Minnesota River drainages in the southern half of the state; the Red River; in northeastern Minnesota, only found in the St. Louis River

Food: insects, crustaceans, fish, some plant debris

Reproduction: in early summer, the male builds a nest in a sheltered area, like undercut banks or behind logs; male guards the eggs and young until the nest is deserted

Record and Average Size: Minnesota state record—38 lb., 44 in.; Average Size—2 to 4 lb. and 12 to 20 in.

Fishing ⬤ Tip: At night, fish in a riffle at the head of a deep hole using frogs as bait. During the day, fish brush piles with cut bait.

Notes: Though not highly respected by many Minnesota anglers, Channel Catfish are hard fighters and considered fine table fare. They were the first widely farmed food fish in the U.S. and are now common in grocery stores and restaurants throughout the country. The Red River supports a world-renowned fishery for trophy Channel Catfish.

Description: color variable, usually mottled yellow or brown; belly cream to yellow; adipose fin; chin barbels; lacks scales; tail squared; head broad and flattened; pronounced underbite

Similar Species: Channel Catfish (pg. 34), Bullheads (pp. 26–30), Tadpole Madtom (pg. 38)

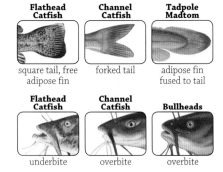

Flathead Catfish	Channel Catfish	Tadpole Madtom
square tail, free adipose fin	forked tail	adipose fin fused to tail

Flathead Catfish	Channel Catfish	Bullheads
underbite	overbite	overbite

FLATHEAD CATFISH
Pylodictis olivaris

Other Names: shovelnose, shovelhead; yellow, mud, pied, or Mississippi cat

Habitat: deep pools of large rivers and impoundments

Range: the Mississippi River watershed into Mexico; large rivers in the Southwest; Minnesota—the Mississippi, Minnesota, and St. Croix Rivers, not above St. Anthony Falls or Taylors Falls; introduced into a few southern Minnesota lakes

Food: fish, crayfish

Reproduction: spawns when water reaches 65 to 80 degrees; male builds and defends nest in hollow logs, undercut banks, or other sheltered areas; large females may lay up to 30,000 eggs

Record and Average Size: Minnesota state record—70 lb.; Average Size—10 to 20 lb. and 20 to 30 in.

Fishing ⬤ Tip: Fish large, active live bait in eddies where small streams enter the main river.

Notes: The Flathead Catfish is a solitary predator that feeds aggressively on live fish. Flatheads spend their days hiding in bank holes and deep pools, then prowl logjams and the shallows for prey at night. Flatheads have been introduced into a few lakes in an attempt to control stunted panfish populations but with poor results. The St. Croix River below Taylors Falls is well known for large flatheads.

STONECAT

TADPOLE MADTOM

Description: Tadpole Madtom—dark olive to brown; dark line on side; large, fleshy head; Stonecat—similar but lacks dark lateral stripe and has protruding upper jaw; both species have adipose fin continuous with tail; lacks scales

Similar Species: Bullheads (pp. 26–30), Catfish (pp. 32–36)

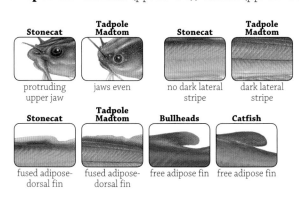

Stonecat	Tadpole Madtom	Stonecat	Tadpole Madtom
protruding upper jaw	jaws even	no dark lateral stripe	dark lateral stripe

Stonecat	Tadpole Madtom	Bullheads	Catfish
fused adipose-dorsal fin	fused adipose-dorsal fin	free adipose fin	free adipose fin

STONECAT *Noturus flavus*

Ictaluridae

TADPOLE MADTOM *Noturus gyrinus*

Other Names: willow cat

Habitat: weedy water near shore; under rocks in stream riffles

Range: eastern U.S.; Minnesota—Stonecats: the St. Croix and Mississippi River systems; Tadpole Madtom: statewide

Food: small invertebrates; algae and other plant matter

Reproduction: both spawn in late spring; female lays eggs under objects such as roots, rocks, logs, or in abandoned crayfish burrows; nest and eggs are guarded by one parent

Record and Average Size: Minnesota state record—none; Average Size—3 to 6 in.

Fishing Tip: Reportedly, damaging the "slime" coating (by rolling them in sand) to make handling easier reduces their effectiveness as bait.

Notes: These are small, secretive, nocturnal fish. Both species have venom glands at the base of the dorsal and pectoral fins. Though not especially dangerous, the venom produces a painful burning sensation, reputed to bring even the hardiest anglers to their knees. Stonecats, and to a lesser degree Tadpole Madtoms, are common baitfish in southern Minnesota. They are favored by many veteran river Walleye anglers, who believe the tough little baitfish are superior to minnows and chubs.

Description: mottled brown with creamy chin and belly; eel-like body; small barbel at each nostril opening; longer barbel on chin; long dorsal fin similar to and just above anal fin

Similar Species: Bowfin (pg. 24), American Eel (pg. 44), Sea Lamprey (pg. 58)

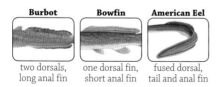

Burbot	Bowfin	American Eel
two dorsals, long anal fin	one dorsal fin, short anal fin	fused dorsal, tail and anal fin

Burbot	Bowfin	Sea Lamprey
small barbel on chin	no barbel on chin	mouth: sucking disk

BURBOT
Lota lota

Other Names: lawyer, eelpout, ling, cusk

Habitat: deep, cold, clear, rock-bottomed lakes and streams

Range: northern North America into Siberia and across northern Europe; Minnesota—most large lakes and rivers north of Mille Lacs Lake; the lower Mississippi River

Food: primarily small fish, fish eggs, clams, and crayfish

Reproduction: pairs to large groups spawn together in mid- to late winter; spawning occurs under the ice, over a sand or gravel bottom in less than 15 feet of water; after spawning, thrashing adults scatter fertilized eggs

Record and Average Size: Minnesota state record—19 lb. 10 oz., 33 in.; Average Size—2 to 8 lb. and 15 to 20 in.

Fishing ◓Tip: Fish a white Marabou jig tipped with a minnow near the bottom.

Notes: A member of the cod family, the Burbot is a coldwater fish, seldom found in fisheries where the water temperature routinely exceeds 69 degrees. It is popular with ice fishermen in some western states and Scandinavia but considered a nuisance by most Minnesota anglers. The flesh is firm, white, and tastes good, but it is not popular.

Description: gray back with purple or bronze reflections; silver sides; white underbelly; humped back; dorsal fin extends from hump to near tail; lateral line runs from head through the tail

Similar Species: White Bass (pg. 158)

Freshwater Drum — triangular tail

White Bass — forked tail

Freshwater Drum — downturned mouth

White Bass — upturned mouth

FRESHWATER DRUM
Aplodinotus grunniens

Other Names: sheepshead, croaker, thunderpumper, grinder, bubbler; commercially marketed as white perch

Habitat: slow to moderate current areas of rivers and streams; shallow lakes with soft bottoms; prefers clean water but tolerates some silt

Range: Canada south through the Midwest into eastern Mexico and to Guatemala; Minnesota—statewide, except the Lake Superior drainage

Food: small fish, insects, crayfish, clams

Reproduction: in May and June, when water temperatures reach about 66 degrees, schools of drum lay eggs near the surface in open water, over sand or gravel; no parental care of fry

Record and Average Size: Minnesota state record—35 lb., 3.2 oz., 36 in.; Average Size—2 to 5 lb. and 10 to 15 in.

Fishing ◖Tip: Fish small white or yellow jigs tipped with a crayfish tail just off the bottom.

Notes: The only freshwater member of a large family of marine fish, the Freshwater Drum gets its name from the grunting noise that males make, primarily to attract females. The sound is produced when specialized muscles rub along the swim bladder. The skull contains two enlarged L-shaped earstones called otoliths, which were once prized as jewelry by Native Americans. The flesh is flaky, white, and tasty but easily dries out when cooked.

Description: dark brown on top with yellow sides and white belly; long snake-like body with a large mouth; gill covers; a continuous dorsal, tail and anal fin

Similar Species: Native Lampreys (pg. 56), Sea Lamprey (pg. 58)

American Eel

one gill cover, pectoral fins

Native Lampreys

seven gill slits, no pectoral fins

American Eel

mouth: jaws

Sea Lamprey

mouth: sucking disk

AMERICAN EEL
Anguilla rostrata

Anguillidae

Other Names: common, Boston, Atlantic, or freshwater eel

Habitat: soft bottoms of medium to large streams, brackish tidewater along Atlantic Coast

Range: the Atlantic Ocean; eastern and central North America and eastern Central America; Minnesota—Mississippi River drainage system and, recently, Lake Superior

Food: insects, crayfish, small fish

Reproduction: a largely "catadromous" species, it spends most of its life in fresh water, returning to the Sargasso Sea in the North Atlantic Ocean to spawn; females lay up to 20 million eggs; adults likely die after spawning

Record and Average Size: Minnesota state record—6 lb., 9 oz., 42 in.; Average Size—2 to 3 lb. and 20 to 30 in.

Fishing ◗ Tip: At night, fish in backwaters just below dams by using nightcrawlers or minnows for bait.

Notes: Leaf-shaped larval eels drift with ocean currents for about a year. When they reach river mouths of North and Central America, they morph into small eels (elvers). Males remain in the estuaries; females migrate upstream. At maturity (up to 20 years), adults return to the Sargasso Sea. Before settlement, eels commonly migrated up the Mississippi River to Minnesota; with the many dams now in place, few eels reach this far inland.

Description: olive to brown with dark spots along sides; long, cylindrical profile; single dorsal fin located just above the anal fin; body is encased in hard, plate-like scales; snout twice as long as head; needle-sharp teeth on both jaws

Similar Species: Shortnose Gar (pg. 48)

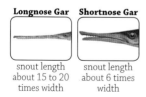

Longnose Gar	Shortnose Gar
snout length about 15 to 20 times width	snout length about 6 times width

LONGNOSE GAR
Lepisosteus osseus

Other Names: garfish

Habitat: quiet waters of larger rivers and lakes

Range: central United States throughout the Mississippi drainage south into Mexico; a few rivers of the Great Lakes; Minnesota—the Mississippi River drainage south of the Twin Cities

Food: minnows and other small fish

Reproduction: lays large, green eggs in weedy shallows when water temperatures reach the high 60s; using a small disk on the snout, a newly-hatched gar attaches to nearby plants, rocks, or branches until its digestive tract develops enough to begin feeding; the large, yellowish-green eggs are toxic to mammals

Record and Average Size: Minnesota state record—16 lb., 12 oz., 53 in.; Average Size—2 to 6 lb. and 24 to 36 in.

Fishing ⬤Tip: To catch gar, you need to entangle their teeth; use spinner jigs made from frayed nylon line.

Notes: The Longnose Gar belongs to a prehistoric family of fish that can breathe air with the aid of a modified swim bladder. This adaptation makes them well suited to survive in increasingly polluted rivers and lakes. They hunt by floating motionless near the surface then making a swift, sideways slash to capture prey. They prefer deep, warm water but often school near the surface. Gars are a valuable asset in controlling the increasing populations of rough fish.

Description: head, back, and sides olive to slate green; long cylindrical body; single dorsal fin located just above the anal fin; body encased in hard plate-like scales; snout one-third longer than its head; needle-sharp teeth on both jaws

Similar Species: Longnose Gar (pg. 46)

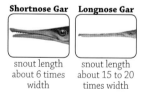

Shortnose Gar	Longnose Gar
snout length about 6 times width	snout length about 15 to 20 times width

SHORTNOSE GAR

Lepisosteus platostomus

Other Names: stubnose, broadnose, or shortbilled gar

Habitat: open water of warm, slow-moving streams, backwaters and shallow lakes

Range: the Mississippi River drainage from the southern Great Lakes to Mexico; Minnesota—common in the southern third of state

Food: minnows and small fish, crayfish

Reproduction: spawns in weedy backwaters when water temperatures reach the mid-60s; the large, yellowish-green eggs are toxic to mammals

Record and Average Size: Minnesota state record—5 lb., 4 oz., 31 in.; Average Size—1 to 2 lb. and 12 to 24 in.

Fishing ⬤ Tip: The Gar responds well to flies made from nylon line when fished near the surface.

Notes: Not as common in Minnesota as the Longnose Gar, the Shortnose Gar prefers somewhat more-active water and can tolerate higher turbidity levels. Like other Gars, it can "gulp" air and withstand very warm and poorly oxygenated water. An ambush predator, it is often seen floating near brush piles and windswept shorelines at the current's edge.

Description: slate-gray scaled body with black and brown spots; steep forehead with bulging eyes; front dorsal fin tinged green with a black spot; a single scallop-shaped dorsal fin

Similar Species: Mottled Sculpin (pg. 112)

Round Goby

Mottled Sculpin

scales on body   lacks scales

ROUND GOBY
Neogobius melanostomus

Other Names: rock goby

Habitat: rocky streams and lake shorelines; brackish coastal shorelines and tributary streams

Range: native to the Black and Caspian seas; invasive in northern Europe and the Great Lakes; Minnesota— Lake Superior and the St. Louis River drainage

Food: mollusks, crustaceans, insects, and fish eggs

Reproduction: spawns several times a year in streams and along rocky shorelines; male protects eggs

Record and Average Size: Minnesota state record—none; Average Size—3 to 12 in.

Fishing ◗ Tip: Check bait pails carefully to ensure that gobies are not introduced to new lakes.

Notes: The Round Goby is an aggressively expanding invasive species that negatively impacts native species. Where it becomes established, native fish populations decrease. Introduced to the Great Lakes in the late 1980s, they are now established in the St. Louis River drainage. Larger gobies are effective predators of zebra mussels, but their overall effect on lake ecology is negative.

Description: silvery with a blue to blue-green metallic shine on back, with silver sides and a white belly; faint dark stripes along sides; dark spot behind the gill and directly above the pectoral fin; large mouth with a protruding lower jaw

Similar Species: Gizzard Shad (pg. 54), Goldeye/Mooneye (pp. 74–76)

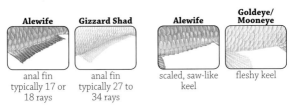

Alewife	Gizzard Shad	Alewife	Goldeye/Mooneye
anal fin typically 17 or 18 rays	anal fin typically 27 to 34 rays	scaled, saw-like keel	fleshy keel

ALEWIFE
Alosa pseudoharengus

Other Names: ellwife, sawbelly, shad or golden shad, big-eyed herring, river herring

Habitat: open water of the Great Lakes and a few inland lakes

Range: the Atlantic Ocean from Labrador to Florida; the St. Lawrence River drainage and the Great Lakes; Minnesota—Lake Superior

Food: zooplankton, filamentous algae

Reproduction: in the Great Lakes, spawning takes place in open water of bays and along protected shorelines during early summer

Record and Average Size: Minnesota state record—none; Average Size—4 to 8 in.

Fishing ⬭ Tip: Alewives, when floated near the bottom close to shore, are a good bait for Lake Trout in the spring.

Notes: When this Atlantic herring reached the eastern Great Lakes, the population exploded. Once sea lamprey populations were under control, the large predators recovered, and the alewife population soon crashed. Not well adapted to freshwater lakes, the alewife is subject to frequent summer kills. Alewives were commercially netted in the eastern Great Lakes and used for animal food.

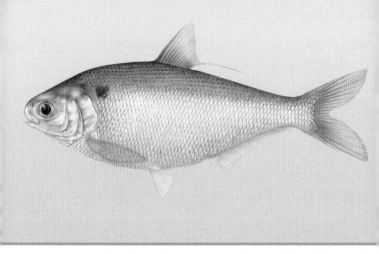

Description: deep, laterally compressed body; silvery blue back with white sides and belly; young fish have a dark spot on shoulder behind the gill; small mouth; last rays of dorsal fin form a long thread

Similar Species: Alewife (pg. 52), Goldeye/Mooneye (pp. 74–76)

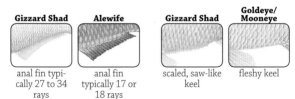

Gizzard Shad	Alewife	Gizzard Shad	Goldeye/Mooneye
anal fin typically 27 to 34 rays	anal fin typically 17 or 18 rays	scaled, saw-like keel	fleshy keel

GIZZARD SHAD
Dorosoma cepedianum

Clupeidae

Other Names: hickory, mud, or jack shad; skipjack

Habitat: large rivers, reservoirs, lakes, swamps, and temporarily flooded pools; brackish and saline waters in coastal areas

Range: the St. Lawrence River and the Great Lakes; Mississippi, the Atlantic, and Gulf Slope drainages from Quebec to Mexico, south to central Florida; Minnesota—the Mississippi, St. Croix, and Minnesota Rivers

Food: herbivorous filter feeder

Reproduction: spawning takes place in tributary streams and along lakeshores in early summer; schooling adults release eggs in open water without regard for individual mates

Record and Average Size: Minnesota state record—none; Average Size—1 to 8 oz. and 4 to 8 in.

Fishing ⬤ Tip: Large Gizzard Shad can be caught by using waxworms in quiet pools at the current's edge.

Notes: The Gizzard Shad is a widespread, prolific fish that is best known as forage for popular game fish. At times gizzard shad can become overabundant and experience large die-offs. The name "gizzard" refers to this shad's long, convoluted intestine that is often packed with sand. Though Gizzard Shad are a management problem at times, they form a valuable link in turning plankton into usable forage for large game fish.

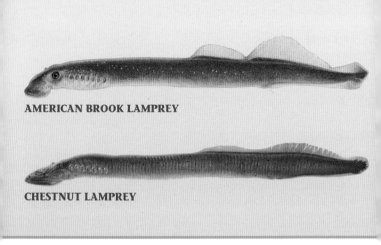

AMERICAN BROOK LAMPREY

CHESTNUT LAMPREY

Description: eel-like body with round, sucking-disk mouth and 7 paired gill openings; dorsal fin is long, extending to the tail; no paired fins

Similar Species: Sea Lamprey (pg. 58) American Eel (pg. 44)

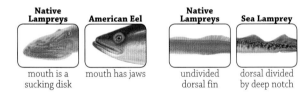

Native Lampreys	American Eel	Native Lampreys	Sea Lamprey
mouth is a sucking disk	mouth has jaws	undivided dorsal fin	dorsal divided by deep notch

NATIVE LAMPREYS

Ichthyomyzon, Lampetra

Petromyzontidae

Other Names: Silver, Chestnut, and American Brook Lamprey

Habitat: juveniles live in the quiet pools of streams and rivers; adults may move into some lakes

Range: fresh water of eastern North America; Minnesota—the Chestnut Lamprey frequents small streams of central and northern Minnesota; the Silver Lamprey is common in larger rivers and streams; the American Brook Lamprey is found only in the southeast, primarily in the Root River

Food: juvenile lampreys are filter feeders in stream bottoms; adults are either parasitic on fish or do not feed

Reproduction: adults build nests in the gravel of streambeds, typically after water temperatures reach about 55 degrees; adults die shortly after spawning

Record and Average Size: Minnesota state record—none; Average Size—6 to 12 in.

Fishing ⬤Tip: Not targeted or used for bait by anglers.

Notes: There are five native lampreys in Minnesota. Adult Chestnut and Silver Lampreys are parasitic, often leaving small, round wounds on their prey. The Brook Lampreys (there are three in all) are not parasitic and do not feed as adults. Minnesota lampreys coexist with other native fish species with little or no effect on populations. Lampreys, generally, are some of Earth's oldest vertebrates, with fossil records dating back 500 million years.

Description: eel-like body; round, sucking-disk mouth; 7 paired gill openings; dorsal fin extends to the tail and is divided into two sections by a deep notch; no paired fins

Similar Species: Native Lampreys (pg. 56), American Eel (pg. 44)

Sea Lamprey

mouth is a sucking disk

American Eel

mouth has jaws

Sea Lamprey

dorsal divided by deep notch

Native Lampreys

undivided dorsal fin

SEA LAMPREY
Petromyzon marinus

Other Names: landlocked or lake lamprey

Habitat: juveniles live in quiet pools of freshwater streams; adults are free-swimming in lakes or oceans

Range: Atlantic Ocean from Greenland to Florida, Norway to the Mediterranean; the Great Lakes; Minnesota—Lake Superior and its tributary streams

Food: juveniles are filter feeders in the bottoms of streams; adult is parasitic on fish, attaching itself using disc-shaped sucker mouth, then using its sharp tongue to rasp through the fish's scales and skin to feed on blood and bodily fluids

Reproduction: both adults build a nest in the gravel of a clear stream, then die shortly after spawning; young remain in streams several years before returning to the lake as adults

Record and Average Size: Minnesota state record—none; Average Size—12 to 24 in.

Fishing ●Tip: Do not return Sea Lampreys to the lake.

Notes: Native to the Atlantic Ocean, the Sea Lamprey entered the Great Lakes via the St. Lawrence Seaway. It was initially blocked by Niagara Falls, but when the Welland Canal allowed it to bypass the falls, it entered the upper Great Lakes. The first specimen was found in Lake Superior in 1936; soon after, Lake Trout and Whitefish populations declined. Control measures, including traps and chemicals, have reduced Sea Lamprey numbers, allowing native fish populations to slowly recover.

Description: dark gray to black back; silver-gray sides with dark blotches; low-set eyes; upturned mouth; tiny body scales, none on head

Similar Species: Common Carp (pg. 62), Silver Carp (pg. 64), Grass Carp (possible in MN)

Bighead Carp	**Common Carp**	**Grass Carp**	**Silver Carp**
small silver scales	large, yellow scales with a dark margin	large, silver scales with a dark margin	small silver scales

Bighead Carp	**Silver Carp**	**Bighead/Silver Carp**	**Common Carp**
keeled belly from pelvic fin to anal fin	keeled belly from gills to anal fin	eyes low on head	eyes high on head

BIGHEAD CARP
Hypophthalmichthys nobilis

Other Names: river carp, lake fish, speckled amur

Habitat: large, warm rivers and connected lakes

Range: Asia; introduced in other parts of the world; Minnesota—a few specimens from southern Minnesota

Food: aquatic vegetation and floating plankton, mostly algae

Reproduction: spawns from late spring to early summer in warm, flowing water

Record and Average Size: Minnesota state record—none; Average Size—5 to 50 lb. and 15 to 25 in.

Fishing ⬭ Tip: As filter feeders, Bighead Carp are targets for bow fishermen but not anglers. They reportedly can be caught with wet flies.

Notes: Bighead Carp are the fourth-most important aquaculture fish in the world. They were introduced to the U.S. to control algae in southern aquaculture ponds and escaped to the Mississippi River. They are now well established south of Minnesota. The Bighead Carp makes high leaps from the water when frightened by boats. Bighead Carp have a mild, pleasant flavor but are bony and are not highly regarded table fare in this country. There is concern that Bighead Carp, if established in Minnesota, could do great harm to the state's fisheries. Any sightings or captures should be reported to the DNR at 651-587-2781 or invasivecarp.dnr@state.mn.us.

Description: brassy yellow to dark-olive back and sides; whitish-yellow belly; round mouth has two pairs of barbels; reddish tail and anal fin; each scale has a dark margin

Similar Species: Bighead Carp (pg. 60), Silver Carp (pg. 64), Grass Carp (possible in MN)

Common Carp

large yellow scales with dark margin

Bighead/Silver Carp

small silver scales

Grass Carp

large silver scales with dark margin

Common Carp

eyes high on head

Bighead/Silver Carp

eyes low on head

COMMON CARP
Cyprinus carpio

Other Names: German, European, mirror or leather carp; buglemouth

Habitat: warm, shallow, quiet, well-vegetated waters of streams and lakes

Range: native to Asia; introduced throughout the world; Minnesota—statewide except the northern lakes region

Food: opportunistic feeder; prefers insect larvae, crustaceans, and mollusks, but at times eats algae and some higher plants

Reproduction: spawns from late spring to early summer in very shallow water at stream and lake edges; very obvious when spawning, with a great deal of splashing

Record and Average Size: Minnesota state record—55 lb., 5 oz., 42 in.; Average Size—3 to 15 lb. and 18 to 24 in.

Fishing ⬤ Tip: For big carp, fish shallow vegetation at night.

Notes: The carp is one of the world's most important freshwater fish. This fast-growing fish provides sport and food for millions of people throughout its range. This Asian minnow was introduced into Europe in the twelfth century but didn't make it to North America until the nineteenth century. Carp are a highly prized sport fish in Europe, but they have not gained the same status in the U.S., even though some line and bowfishers do enthusiastically fish for carp.

Description: dark green back; silver sides with a cross-hatched pattern; upturned mouth; eyes far forward and low on head; tiny trout-like scales; no scales on head

Similar Species: Bighead Carp (pg. 60), Common Carp (pg. 62), Grass Carp (possible in Minnesota)

Silver Carp

small silver scales

Bighead Carp

small silver scales

Common Carp

large yellow scales with dark margin

Grass Carp

large silver scales with dark margin

Silver Carp

keeled belly from gills to anal fin

Bighead Carp

keeled belly from pelvic fin to anal fin

Silver/Bighead Carp

eyes low on head, mouth lacks barbels

Common Carp

eyes high on head, mouth has barbels

SILVER CARP
Hypophthalmichthys molitrix

Other Names: shiner carp

Habitat: quiet waters of large, warm rivers and connected lakes and ponds

Range: Asia; introduced elsewhere; Minnesota—a few have been found in the St. Croix and Mississippi rivers

Food: floating algae and small aquatic vegetation

Reproduction: spawns from late spring to early summer in backwaters of large to mid-size streams

Record and Average Size: Minnesota state record—none; Average Size—5 to 20 lb. and 20 to 30 in.

Fishing ⬤ Tip: Algae feeders, they are targets for bowfishers but not anglers. Reportedly they can be caught on hook and line by floating small baits, like waxworms, in feeding schools.

Notes: Silver Carp were introduced to Arkansas in the early 1970s to control algae in aquaculture ponds and sewage lagoons, but they then escaped to the Mississippi River. Large breeding populations are well established in the Ohio, Illinois, and lower Mississippi Rivers. Combined with Bighead Carp, they are the predominant fish in some areas and have had a very negative effect on river ecology. They have limited food value in this country but are an important food source elsewhere. The Silver Carp makes high leaps from the water when frightened by boats. Any sightings or captures should be reported to the DNR at 651-587-2781 or invasivecarp.dnr@state.mn.us.

Description: gray to olive brown, often with a dark stripe on side and black spot at the base of tail; red spot behind eye; breeding males develop horn-like tubercles on the head

Similar Species: Fathead Minnow (pg. 70), Creek Chub

Hornyhead Chub

downturned mouth extends to eye

Fathead Minnow

upturned mouth does not extend to eye

Creek Chub

mouth extends to middle of eye

HORNYHEAD CHUB
Nocomis biguttatus

Cyprinidae

Other Names: redtail, horned, or river chub

Habitat: small to medium-size streams; occasionally found in lakes near stream mouths

Range: northern Midwest through the Great Lakes region; Minnesota—statewide

Food: small aquatic invertebrates, zooplankton

Reproduction: in late spring, male excavates a 1- to 3-foot-diameter pit in a gravelly stream riffle, then fills it with small stones creating a 6- to 8-inch-high mound; females lay eggs on the mound; male covers fertilized eggs with gravel; other species such as Common Shiner may also use the mound for spawning

Record and Average Size: Minnesota state record—none; Average Size—4 to 12 in.

Fishing ⬤ Tip: Chubs are an excellent bait for walleyes in the fall.

Notes: Minnesota's six chubs (Creek, Hornyhead, Gravel, Lake, Silver, and Speckled) are our largest native minnows. The Creek and Hornyhead grow to a foot long and can be caught with hook and line. The Hornyhead is a common bait minnow, often called Redtail Chub. Due to high demand, anglers sometimes pay over a dollar per fish, making it costlier per pound than lobster. Recently, habitat loss and harvest pressure by bait dealers have caused populations to decline.

Description: moderately dark back; two broad lateral bands on tan background; in breeding males the tan turns orange and the belly becomes bright red or orange; blunt nose

Similar Species: Southern Redbelly Dace, Finescale Dace

Northern Redbelly Dace

curved mouth, lower jaw slightly ahead of upper

Southern Redbelly Dace

straight mouth, upper jaw slightly ahead of the lower

Northern Redbelly Dace

two dark lateral stripes

Finescale Dace

single dark lateral stripe

NORTHERN REDBELLY DACE

Phoxinus eos

Other Names: redbelly, leatherback, yellow-belly dace

Habitat: small streams and bog lakes

Range: Northwest Territories to Hudson Bay, northeastern U.S., and eastern Canada; Minnesota—all river drainages; more common in northern two-thirds of state

Food: plant material

Reproduction: from May to early August, a single female accompanied by several males will dart among masses of filamentous algae, laying 5 to 30 non-adhesive eggs at a time; males fertilize the eggs, which hatch in 8 to 10 days with no parental care

Record and Average Size: Minnesota state record—none; Average Size—2 to 3 in.

Fishing ⬤ Tip: Dace are average as bait minnows. They survive in the bait pail pretty well but not long once on the hook.

Notes: Six species of Minnesota minnows are referred to as Daces: the Finescale, Longnose, Northern Redbelly, Pearl, Redside, and Southern Redbelly. Daces are small fish that live in a variety of habitats. The Northern Redbelly Dace is a hardy fish often found in the acid water of bog-stained lakes, beaver ponds, and small streams. Breeding males are one of Minnesota's brightest-colored fish and surpass many aquarium fish in beauty. Northern Redbelly Dace often hybridize with other species and sometimes form all-female populations.

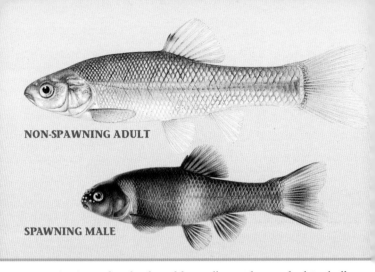

NON-SPAWNING ADULT

SPAWNING MALE

Description: olive back, golden yellow sides, and white belly; dark lateral line widens to spot at base of tail; rounded snout and fins; no scales on head; dark blotch on dorsal fin

Similar Species: Hornyhead Chub (pg. 66), Creek Chub

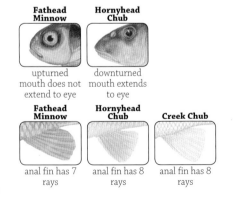

Fathead Minnow

upturned mouth does not extend to eye

Hornyhead Chub

downturned mouth extends to eye

Fathead Minnow

anal fin has 7 rays

Hornyhead Chub

anal fin has 8 rays

Creek Chub

anal fin has 8 rays

FATHEAD MINNOW

Pimephales promelas

Cyprinidae

Other Names: fathead, blackhead, tuffy, mudminnow

Habitat: streams, ponds, and lakes, particularly shallow, weedy, or turbid areas lacking predators

Range: east of the Rocky Mountains in the U.S. and Canada; Minnesota—statewide

Food: primarily herbivorous, but will eat insects and copepods

Reproduction: from the time water temperatures reach 60 degrees in spring through August, male prepares nest under rocks and sticks; female enters, turns upside down, and lays adhesive eggs on the overhead object; after the female leaves, the male fertilizes the eggs, which it then guards, fans with its fins, and massages with a special, mucus-like pad on its back

Record and Average Size: Minnesota state record—none; Average Size—1 to 2 in.

Fishing ⬤ Tip: Some anglers report less luck when using breeding male fatheads as bait, perhaps due to their color or a differing scent.

Notes: Minnows are small fish, not young individuals of larger species. The fathead is one of our most numerous and widespread fish in Minnesota, and it is commonly used as bait. It is hardy and withstands extremely low oxygen levels—both in the wild and in bait buckets. Prior to spawning, the male undergoes a variety of changes, developing a dark coloration, breeding tubercles on its head that resemble small horns, and a mucus-like pad on its back.

GOLDEN SHINER

COMMON SHINER

Description: silver body with a dark green back, often with a
dark body stripe; breeding males have bluish heads and rosy
pink body and fins

Similar Species: Golden Shiner, Hornyhead Chub

8 to 10 rays on
anal fin
(usually 9)

11 to 15 rays
on anal fin

eye large in
relation to the
head

eye small in
relation to head

Cyprinidae

COMMON SHINER
Luxilus cornutus

Other Names: common, eastern, creek, or redfin shiner

Habitat: lakes, rivers, and streams; most common in pools of streams and small rivers

Range: Midwest through the eastern U.S. and Canada; Minnesota—statewide

Food: small insects, algae, zooplankton

Reproduction: beginning in late May, male prepares nest of small stones and gravel at the head of a stream riffle; females are courted with great flourish

Record and Average Size: Minnesota state record—none; Average Size—3 to 12 in.

Fishing ⬤ Tip: Large Common Shiners can be caught on dry flies and are occasionally eaten; though not as meaty as panfish, they are every bit as tenacious when hooked.

Notes: There are nearly 20 minnows in Minnesota known as shiners, and many of them are very hard to tell apart. Not all shiners are as flashy as the name indicates. Some are dull-colored and show almost no silver on the sides. The Common Shiner is one of the larger native Minnesota minnows, occasionally reaching 12 inches in length. The Common Shiner has now replaced the Golden Shiner as the common bait shiner, though it seems somewhat less hardy once on the hook.

Description: dark green to dark blue back and upper sides; bright silver or golden sides; large yellow-tinged eye; large scales; thin body flattened from side to side with a sharp scale ridge (keel) from throat to pelvic fin; forward-facing mouth with small teeth

Similar Species: Mooneye (pg. 76), Gizzard Shad (pg. 54)

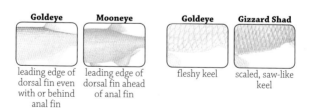

Goldeye	Mooneye		Goldeye	Gizzard Shad
leading edge of dorsal fin even with or behind anal fin	leading edge of dorsal fin ahead of anal fin		fleshy keel	scaled, saw-like keel

GOLDEYE
Hiodon alosoides

Other Names: Winnipeg or western goldeye; toothed or yellow herring

Habitat: large lakes and quiet backwaters of large, turbid streams and rivers

Range: the Hudson Bay drainage south through the Ohio and Mississippi River drainages to Tennessee; Minnesota—statewide except the Lake Superior drainage

Food: insects, small fish, crayfish, snails

Reproduction: spawning takes place in turbid pools and backwaters when water temperatures reach the mid-50s

Record and Average Size: Minnesota state record—2 lb., 13.1 oz., 20.1 in.; Average Size—8 to 20 oz. and 10 to 17 in.

Fishing ⬭ Tip: While not often an angler's target, Goldeyes readily take flies and small lures and are frequently caught while fishing for other species. It is not a very strong fighter.

Notes: The Goldeye's large yellow eye is an adaptation for low-light conditions and enables it to feed at night and navigate dark, silty waters. They feed near the surface in quiet pools and are often found with Mooneyes. Harvested commercially from large Canadian lakes for 150 years, they were served on the Canadian Pacific Railway as "Winnipeg Smoked Goldeye." They are still fairly common in the Mississippi and St. Croix rivers (below Taylors Falls in the St. Croix).

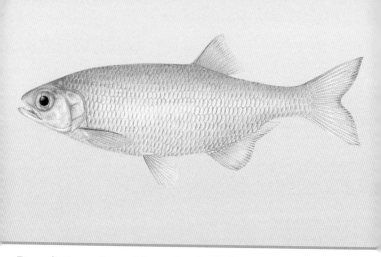

Description: silver with an olive back; large scales on the body but none on the head; large, white eye more than one-third the width of head; thin body with a sharp scaleless keel between pelvic and anal fins

Similar Species: Goldeye (pg. 74), Gizzard Shad (pg. 54)

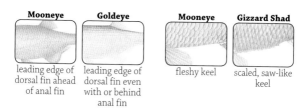

Mooneye	Goldeye	Mooneye	Gizzard Shad
leading edge of dorsal fin ahead of anal fin	leading edge of dorsal fin even with or behind anal fin	fleshy keel	scaled, saw-like keel

MOONEYE
Hiodon tergisus

Other Names: white shad, slicker, toothed herring, river whitefish

Habitat: clear, quiet waters of large lakes and the backwaters of large streams

Range: the Hudson Bay drainage east to the St. Lawrence drainage, through the Mississippi drainage south into Arkansas and Alabama; Minnesota—statewide except the Lake Superior drainage

Food: insects, small fish, crayfish, snails

Reproduction: spawning takes place in clear backwaters and over rocks in areas with fast-moving water when water temperatures reach the mid-50s; a single female may release up to 20,000 gelatin-covered eggs

Record and Average Size: Minnesota state record—1 lb., 15 oz., 16.5 in.; Average Size—12 to 16 oz. and 10 to 12 in.

Fishing ◗Tip: Mooneyes will take flies, but they are not great fighters.

Notes: The Mooneye is a flashy fish that jumps repeatedly when hooked. However, it is bony, with little meat except along the back. It commonly feeds on insects at or near the surface in slack waters of large lakes and rivers. Mooneyes prefer cleaner water than Goldeyes, and it is becoming less common due to the siltation of many streams. Though small, it is related to the South American Arapaima, the world's largest scaled freshwater fish.

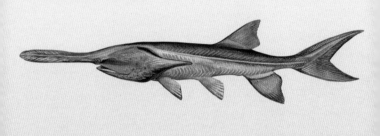

Description: large, gray scaleless body; snout protrudes into a large paddle; shark-like forked tail; gill cover extends into long, pointed flaps

Similar Species: Channel Catfish (pg. 34), Blue Catfish (pg. 32)

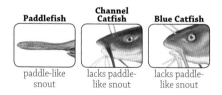

Paddlefish	**Channel Catfish**	**Blue Catfish**
paddle-like snout	lacks paddle-like snout	lacks paddle-like snout

PADDLEFISH
Polyodon spathula

Other Names: spoonbill cat, duckbill

Habitat: deep pools of large rivers and their connecting lakes

Range: large rivers in the Mississippi drainage; Minnesota—the lower Mississippi and the St. Croix Rivers; most common in Lake St. Croix and Lake Pepin

Food: free-swimming plankton

Reproduction: spawning takes place in the spring with rising water levels; adults migrate from lakes and rivers into streams; breeding schools gather to release eggs over large gravel bars, typically in less than 10 feet of water

Record and Average Size: Minnesota state record—none; Average size—20 to 40 lb. and 24 to 36 in.

Fishing ⬤ Tip: In some states there is a snagging season for Paddlefish but not in Minnesota.

Notes: This prehistoric fish is very shark-like in terms of anatomy. Its only close relative is found in China's Yangtze River. The Paddlefish has a large mouth but no teeth, and it feeds entirely on plankton. The function of its namesake paddle is not well understood, but it is not used to dig in the mud. Scientists believe special sensors in the snout help the Paddlefish detect tiny electrical currents created by the plankton on which it feeds. With the increased pollution and silting-in of the Mississippi River, the Paddlefish is now rare in Minnesota, but it was once common and a prized food fish.

IOWA DARTER

JOHNNY DARTER

Description: Iowa Darter—brown back with faint blotches; sides have 9 to 12 vertical bars; dark spot under eye; bars are more pronounced and colors brighter in breeding males; Johnny Darter—tan to olive back and upper sides with dark blotches and speckling; sides tan to golden with X, Y, and W patterns; breeding males dark with black bars

Similar Species: Iowa Darter; Johnny Darter

Iowa Darter **Johnny Darter**

blotches or bars on sides

X, Y, and W markings on sides

IOWA DARTER *Etheostoma exile*
JOHNNY DARTER *Etheostoma nigrum*

Other Names: red-sided, yellowbelly, or weed darter

Habitat: Iowa Darters inhabit slow-flowing streams and lakes that have some vegetation or an algae mat; Johnny Darters are found in most rivers, streams, and lakes

Range: the Rockies east across Canada and the U.S. through the Great Lakes region; Minnesota—both found statewide

Food: waterfleas, insect larvae

Reproduction: in May and June, males migrate to shore-lines to establish breeding areas; females move from territory to territory, spawning with several males; each sequence produces 7 to 10 eggs, which sink and attach to the bottom

Record and Average Size: Minnesota state record—none; Average Size—2 to 4 in.

Fishing ⬤ Tip: Neither species is a good bait minnow.

Notes: Relatives of Yellow Perch and Walleyes, darters are primarily stream fish that live among rocks in fast currents. Their small swim bladders allow them to sink rapidly to the bottom after making a quick "dart," thus avoiding being swept away by the current. The Johnny is the most common species and is found in most lakes, streams, and rivers statewide. The Iowa Darter is a species of slow-moving streams and lakes; it inhabits weedy shorelines. They are hard to see when still, but easy to spot when making a quick dart to a new resting place, where they perch on their pectoral fins. Iowa Darters make fine aquarium fish but require live food.

81

Description: olive or golden brown back; large continuous spiny dorsal fin; spots between dorsal spines; large spine on pelvic fins; scaleless head

Similar Species: Yellow Perch (pg. 88); Trout-Perch (pg. 164)

Ruffe	**Yellow Perch**	**Trout-Perch**
continuous dorsal fin, spots between rays	separated dorsal fin, no spots	single dorsal fin, no spots

RUFFE

Gymnocephalus cernuus

Other Names: blacktail, pope, redfin darter, river ruffe

Habitat: bottom dweller of streams and lakes (down to about 300 feet)

Range: temperate regions of Europe and Asia; western Great Lakes; Minnesota—Lake Superior and the St. Louis River drainage

Food: mostly insect larvae

Reproduction: spawns April through June in rocky shallows; aggressive breeder that displaces native fish; may have two broods per year

Record and Average Size: Minnesota state record—none; Average Size—3 to 10 in.

Fishing ⬤ Tip: Ruffe should never be used as bait, and care should be taken to not spread them to other lakes or streams.

Notes: The Ruffe is a very aggressive invasive species that was introduced to the Great Lakes from ship ballast water in the 1980s. It is now the most populous fish in the St. Louis River, disrupting native ecology. Where it is established in both Europe and the U. S., native fish populations are declining. The DNR should be notified if Ruffe are found anywhere outside of Lake Superior and the St. Louis River.

SAUGER

SAUGEYE

Description: slender body; gray to dark silver or yellowish brown with dark blotches on sides; black spots on spiny dorsal fin; may exhibit some white on lower margin of tail, but lacks prominent white spot found on Walleyes

Similar Species: Walleye (pg. 86), Saugeye

Sauger	Saugeye	Walleye
dorsal has distinct circular spots, no blotch on rear base	dorsal has distinct spots and blotch at rear base	dorsal has indistinct spots, dark blotch on rear base
cheeks rough with few scales	cheeks rough with scales	cheeks smooth with few scales

SAUGER
Sander canadensis

Other Names: sand pike, spotfin pike, river pike, jackfish, jack salmon

Habitat: large lakes and rivers

Range: Canada and the northern U.S.; the Mississippi, Missouri, Ohio, and Tennessee River drainages; Minnesota—large northern lakes, the St. Croix River south of Taylors Falls, the lower Minnesota River, and the Mississippi River south of St. Anthony Falls

Food: small fish, aquatic insects, crayfish

Reproduction: spawns in April and May as water approaches 50 degrees; adults move into the shallow waters of tributaries and headwaters to randomly deposit eggs over gravel beds

Record and Average Size: Minnesota state record—6 lb., 23.8 in.; Average Size—8 oz. to 2 lb. and 10 to 15 in.

Fishing ⬤ Tip: Compared to walleyes, Saugers are slightly more aggressive daytime feeders; they also respond to a little faster retrieve and brighter colors during summer river fishing.

Notes: Though the Sauger is the Walleye's smaller cousin, it is a big-water fish primarily found in large lakes and rivers. It is slow-growing, often reaching only 2 pounds in 20 years. The Sauger is an important sport fish, summer and winter, in the lower Mississippi River, Lake of the Woods, and Rainy Lake. Saugeye is a natural hybrid of Walleye and Sauger and common in Lake of the Woods and the lower Mississippi River.

Description: long, round body; dark silver or golden to dark olive brown in color; spines in both first dorsal and anal fin; sharp canine teeth; dark spot at base of the three last spines in the dorsal fin; white spot on bottom lobe of tail

Similar Species: Sauger (pg. 84), Saugeye

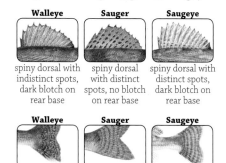

Walleye	Sauger	Saugeye
spiny dorsal with indistinct spots, dark blotch on rear base	spiny dorsal with distinct spots, no blotch on rear base	spiny dorsal with distinct spots, dark blotch on rear base

Walleye	Sauger	Saugeye
white spot on bottom lobe of tail	no white spot on bottom of tail	no white spot on bottom of tail

WALLEYE
Sander vitreus

Percidae

Other Names: marble-eyes, 'eye, walter, walleyed pike, jack, jackfish, pickerel

Habitat: lakes, rivers, and streams; abundant in some very large lakes

Range: northern states and Canada, now widely stocked in the U.S.; Minnesota—statewide

Food: mainly small fish, but also eats insects, crayfish, leeches, and frogs

Reproduction: spawning takes place in tributary streams or rocky lake shoals when spring water temperatures reach 45 to 50 degrees; no parental care

Record and Average Size: Minnesota state record—17 lb., 8 oz., 36.8 in.; Average Size—1 to 3 lb. and 10 to 18 in.

Fishing Tip: Casting imitation crawfish lures (the kind used for bass) into rocky shorelines at night can be very effective for large Walleyes.

Notes: Minnesota's state fish, the Walleye is revered by Minnesota anglers. A dogged opponent, but not a spectacular fighter or jumper, the Walleye is at the top of the list of North American fish when it reaches the table. A reflective layer of pigment in the eye, the tapetum lucidum, allows Walleyes, and their cousin, Saugers, to see well in low-light conditions. As a result, Walleyes are most active at dusk, dawn, night, and under low-light conditions, such as choppy waves and cloudy skies.

Description: 6 to 9 dark, vertical bars on bright yellowish green to orange background; long dorsal fin with two distinct lobes; lower fins have a yellow to orange tinge

Similar Species: Trout-Perch (pg. 164), Walleye (pg. 86)

Yellow Perch	Trout-Perch	Yellow Perch	Walleye
no adipose fin	adipose fin	lacks prominent white spot on tail	prominent white spot on tail

YELLOW PERCH
Perca flavescens

Other Names: ringed, striped, or jack perch, green hornet

Habitat: lakes and streams; prefers clear, open water

Range: northern U.S. and southern Canada; Minnesota—statewide

Food: small fish, insects, snails, leeches, and crayfish

Reproduction: spawns at night in shallow, weedy areas soon after ice-out when water warms to 45 degrees; female drapes gelatinous ribbons of eggs over submerged vegetation

Record and Average Size: Minnesota state record—3 lb., 4 oz., Average Size—6 to 10 oz. and 6 to 10 in.

Fishing ⬤ Tip: Perch are very sensitive to color, so when fishing is slow, consider changing jig color.

Notes: The Yellow Perch is very common and prolific in large north-central lakes. Small, bait-stealing perch are considered a nuisance, but individuals that reach 10 inches or more are popular with many anglers. Perch travel in schools of about the same age class and size, so when a group of actively feeding fish is located, large numbers can often be caught. Perch are an important link in the food web, serving as forage for larger sport fish. In turn, overfishing of these top predators can lead to a population of "stunted," or undersized perch.

MUSKELLUNGE

TIGER MUSKIE

Description: torpedo-shaped body; dorsal fin near tail; sides typically silver to silver-green with dark spots or bars on light background; pointed lobes on tail and paired fins; lower half of gill cover has no scales

Similar Species: Northern Pike (pg. 92), Tiger Muskie

Muskellunge	**Northern Pike**
dark marks on light background	light marks on dark background

Muskellunge	**Northern Pike**
6 or more pores on each side under the jaw	5 or fewer pores each side under the jaw

Muskellunge	**Northern Pike**	**Tiger Muskie**
pointed tail	rounded tail	rounded tail

MUSKELLUNGE
Esox masquinongy

Other Names: musky, muskie, 'ski, lunge

Habitat: large, clear lakes with extensive weedbeds; medium to large rivers with slow currents and deep pools

Range: the Great Lakes east to Maine, south through the Ohio River drainage to Tennessee; Minnesota—native to the Rainy River and Mississippi drainages, introduced statewide

Food: small fish; occasionally muskrats and ducklings

Reproduction: spawns mid-April to May when water temperatures reach 50–60 degrees; lays eggs in dead vegetation in tributaries or shallow bays with mucky bottoms; male and female swim side by side for several hundred yards; in the process, eggs are fertilized and deposited

Record and Average Size: Minnesota state record—54 lb., 56 in.; Average Size—10 to 20 lb. and 30 to 40 in.

Fishing ⬯Tip: Using a bobber, fish with medium-size sucker minnows in open holes in large weedbeds.

Notes: Muskies are legendary among anglers for their sheer size, power, and explosive strikes. They are thinly dispersed (typically one fish every 2 or 3 acres), and they are hard to fool with live bait or lures. Studies in Wisconsin have shown that, on average, it takes 50 hours of fishing to catch a 40-inch fish. Muskies hybridize with Northern Pike to produce the Tiger Muskellunge. Because they are less aggressive in rearing tanks, Tiger Muskies are commonly stocked in Minnesota lakes.

Description: long body with dorsal fin near the tail; head is long and flattened in front, forming a duck-like snout; dark green back; light green sides with bean-shaped light spots; Silver Pike are a rare, silver-colored mutation of Northern Pike

Similar Species: Muskellunge (pg. 90), Tiger Muskie

Northern Pike

Muskellunge

light marks on dark background

dark marks on light background

Northern Pike

Muskellunge

5 or fewer pores on each side under the jaw

6 or more pores on each side under the jaw

Northern Pike

Muskellunge

Tiger Muskie

rounded tail

pointed tail

rounded tail

NORTHERN PIKE
Esox lucius

Esocidae

Other Names: pickerel, jack, gator, hammerhandle, snot rocket

Habitat: lakes, ponds, streams, and rivers; often found near weeds; small pike tolerate water temperatures up to 70 degrees, but larger fish prefer cooler water, 55 degrees or less

Range: northern Europe, Asia, and North America; Minnesota—statewide

Food: small fish, crayfish, and occasionally frogs

Reproduction: late March to early April in tributaries and marshes when water reaches 34–40 degrees; attended by one to three males, female deposits eggs in shallow vegetation

Record and Average Size: Minnesota state record—45 lb., 12 oz., Average Size—2 to 10 lb. and 24 to 30 in.

Fishing ⬭ Tip: During the first couple of weeks of the fishing season, floating dead sucker minnows near the bottom in weedy shallows is deadly for big pike.

Notes: Our most widespread game fish, Northern Pike eagerly hit natural and artificial baits and then fight hard when hooked. They are of good table quality, but they are bony. The pike's firm, white flesh can acquire a "fishy" taste if it comes in contact with the pike's outer slime. A daytime ambush feeder, Northerns often lie in wait in weedy cover, capturing prey with a fast lunge. Big fish often break the line at the boat by employing the same fast lunge.

Description: back is olive or blue-gray to black with worm-like markings; sides bronze to olive with red spots tinged light brown; lower fins red-orange with white leading edge; tail squared or slightly forked

Similar Species: Brown Trout (pg. 96), Rainbow Trout (pg. 100), Lake Trout (pg. 98), Splake

Brook Trout

worm-like marks, red spots

Brown Trout

large dark spots, small red dots

Rainbow Trout

pink stripe on silver body

Lake Trout

sides lack red spots

Brook Trout

tail square to slightly forked

Lake Trout

tail deeply forked

Splake

tail moderately forked

BROOK TROUT
Salvelinus fontinalis

Salmonidae

Other Names: speckled, squaretail, or coaster trout; brookie

Habitat: cool, clear streams and small lakes with sand or gravel bottoms and moderate vegetation; coastal in large lakes; prefers water temperatures of 50 to 60 degrees or below

Range: Great Lakes region north to Labrador, south through the Appalachians to Georgia; introduced into the western U.S., Canada, Europe, and South America; Minnesota—statewide

Food: insects, small fish, leeches, crustaceans

Reproduction: spawns in late fall when water temperatures reach 40–49 degrees; spawning takes place on gravel bars in stream riffles and in lakes where springs aerate eggs; female builds 4- to 12-inch-deep nest (male may guard it during construction) in gravel, then buries fertilized eggs

Record and Average Size: Minnesota state record—6 lb., 5 oz., 24 in.; Average Size—8 to 16 oz. and 8 to 10 in.

Fishing ⬤ Tip: Fish along the shore of Lake Superior in the evening or early morning with brown or green poppers. Be very quiet, and don't cast a shadow on the water.

Notes: Native to Minnesota's cool, clear streams, this beautiful little trout is prized by trout fishermen because of its voracious appetite, strong runs, and delicate flavor. Brook Trout were introduced into remote Minnesota streams by loggers in the 1800s and, more recently, by the DNR. The state supports a stable Brook Trout fishery, but it is susceptible to stream degradation and climate change, particularly warming waters.

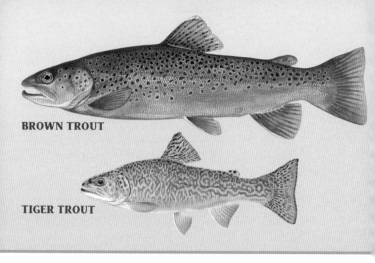

BROWN TROUT

TIGER TROUT

Description: golden brown to olive back and sides; large dark spots on sides, dorsal fin, and sometimes upper lobe of tail; red spots with light halos scattered along sides

Similar Species: Rainbow Trout (pg. 100), Lake Trout (pg. 98), Brook Trout (pg. 94), Tiger Trout

Brown Trout	Rainbow Trout	Lake Trout
dark spots on brown or olive	pink stripe on silvery body	white spots on dark background

Brown Trout	Brook Trout	Tiger Trout
lacks worm-like markings	worm-like markings on back	worm-like markings on back and sides

Salmonidae

BROWN TROUT
Salmo trutta

Other Names: German brown, Loch Leven, or spotted trout

Habitat: open ocean near its spawning streams and clear, cold, gravel-bottomed streams; shallow areas of large lakes

Range: native to Europe from the Mediterranean to Arctic Norway and Siberia; widely introduced worldwide; Minnesota—statewide

Food: insects, crayfish, small fish

Reproduction: spawns October through December in stream headwaters and tributaries; stream mouths are used when migration is blocked; female fans out saucer-shaped nest, which male guards until spawning; female covers eggs

Record and Average Size: Minnesota State Record—16 lb., 12 oz., 31.4 in.; Average Size—2 to 6 lb. and 10 to 20 in.

Fishing ⬤ Tip: A very small spinner tied just ahead of a black-and-gray streamer will sometimes wake up sluggish Brown Trout.

Notes: This European trout was brought to North America in 1883 and Minnesota shortly after. A favorite of anglers, it is a secretive, elusive fish that fights hard and has a fine, delicate flavor. It often feeds aggressively on cloudy, rainy days and at night. It tolerates warmer, cloudier water than other trout, allowing it to live in the lower reaches of coldwater streams. Though it can survive in 80-degree water for a short time, it prefers the 50s to lower 60s. Hybridizes with Brook Trout to produce the sterile Tiger Trout.

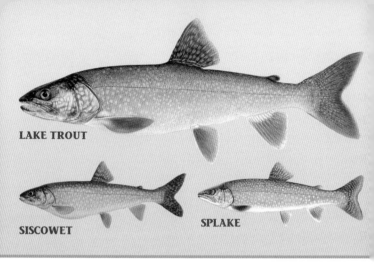

LAKE TROUT

SISCOWET

SPLAKE

Description: dark gray to gray-green on head, back, top fins, and tail; white spots on sides and unpaired fins; deeply forked tail; inside of mouth is white

Similar Species: Brook Trout (pg. 94), Splake, Siscowet

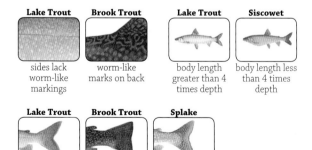

Lake Trout	Brook Trout	Lake Trout	Siscowet
sides lack worm-like markings	worm-like marks on back	body length greater than 4 times depth	body length less than 4 times depth

Lake Trout	Brook Trout	Splake
tail deeply forked	tail square to slightly forked	tail moderately forked

LAKE TROUT
Salvelinus namaycush

Other Names: togue, mackinaw, great gray trout, laker

Habitat: cold (less than 65 degrees), oxygen-rich waters of deep, clear, infertile lakes

Range: the Great Lakes north through Canada and the northeastern U.S.; stocked in some Rocky Mountain lakes; Minnesota—Lake Superior and some deep northern lakes

Food: small fish, insects

Reproduction: females scatter eggs over rocky lake bottoms when the fall water temperatures get below 50 degrees

Record and Average Size: Minnesota state record—43 lb., 8 oz.; Average Size—2 to 10 lb. and 15 to 20 in.

Fishing ⬭ Tip: In early spring, Lake Trout can be caught almost anywhere along Lake Superior shores by floating dead smelt just off the bottom.

Notes: The Lake Trout is native to Minnesota and prized for sport and food. The Lake Superior population was decimated in the 1950s by overfishing and the introduction of the Sea Lamprey. Stocking and lamprey control has restored levels that support sport fishing. In summer, Lake Trout are caught by deep trolling, or by "surf" fishing the mouths of North Shore streams. Lake Trout hybridizes with Brook Trout to produce Splake. A deep-bodied, high-fat subspecies called the Siscowet or the Fat Lake Trout (*Salvelinus namaycush siscowet*) inhabits the frigid, 300- to 600-foot depths of Lake Superior.

Description: blue-green to brown head and back; silver lower sides, often with pink to rose stripe; sides, back, dorsal fins, and tail are covered with small black spots

Similar Species: Brown Trout (pg. 96), Brook Trout (pg. 94), Pink Salmon (pg. 106), Chinook Salmon (pg. 102)

Rainbow Trout
pinkish stripe on silvery body

Brown Trout
sides lack pinkish stripe

Rainbow Trout
lacks worm-like markings

Brook Trout
worm-like marks on back

Rainbow Trout
white mouth

Pink Salmon
dark tongue and jaw tip

Chinook Salmon
black or dark gray mouth

RAINBOW TROUT
Oncorhynchus mykiss

Salmonidae

Other Names: steelhead, Pacific trout, silver trout, 'bow

Habitat: prefers whitewater in cool streams and coastal regions of large lakes; tolerates smaller cool, clear lakes

Range: Pacific Ocean and coastal streams from Mexico to Alaska and northeast Russia; introduced worldwide; Minnesota—statewide

Food: insects, small crustaceans, and fish

Reproduction: predominantly a spring spawner, but some fall-spawning varieties have been introduced into the state; females build nest in well-aerated gravel in both streams and lakes

Record and Average Size: Minnesota state record—16 lb., 6 oz., 33 in.; Average Size—8 oz. to 6 lb. and 10 to 20 in.

Fishing ⬭Tip: In inland lakes stocked with trout, small red spinners tipped with a minnow work well.

Notes: This Pacific trout was one of the first non-native fish stocked in Minnesota, more than 100 years ago. It is known for acrobatic battles and excellent table quality. Reproduces in some streams and lakes, but much of the state's fishery is maintained by stocking. Steelheads are Rainbow Trout that spend their life in the open ocean or lakes, then migrate upstream to spawn. Kamloops (also known as loopers) are a strain of steelhead that were used in some stocking programs on Lake Superior.

Description: iridescent green to blue-green back and upper sides, silver below lateral line; small spots on back and tail; inside of mouth is dark; breeding males are olive brown to purple with pronounced kype (hooked snout)

Similar Species: Coho Salmon (pg. 104), Pink Salmon (pg. 106), Rainbow Trout (pg. 100)

Chinook Salmon	**Coho Salmon**	**Pink Salmon**
small spots throughout tail	spots only in top half of tail	eye-size spots throughout tail

Chinook Salmon	**Coho Salmon**	**Rainbow Trout**
inside of mouth is dark	inside of mouth is gray	inside of mouth is white

CHINOOK SALMON
Oncorhynchus tshawytscha

Other Names: king, spring salmon, tyee, quinnat, black mouth

Habitat: open ocean, large clear gravel-bottomed rivers, and large lakes

Range: Pacific Ocean north from California to Japan; introduced to the Atlantic Coast in Maine and Great Lakes; Minnesota—Lake Superior

Food: fish, some crustaceans

Reproduction: Chinooks in the Great Lakes mature in 3 to 5 years; in October and November they migrate up streams to attempt nesting on gravel bars; adults die shortly after

Record and Average Size: Minnesota state record—33 lb., 4 oz., 44.75 in.; Average Size—8 to 15 lb. and 24 to 30 in.

Fishing Tip: Salmon seem to be picky about color; when the bite is slow, keep changing lure color.

Notes: The largest member of the salmon family, the Chinook may reach 40 pounds in landlocked lakes and can get much larger in the Pacific; the late-maturing strain that spawns in Alaska's Kenai River often tops 60 pounds and produced the world record of nearly 100 pounds. A renowned fighter prized as table fare, the Chinook is popular with anglers. Sporadic attempts to stock the Chinook in inland Minnesota lakes have failed. Chinooks now reproduce naturally in Lake Superior.

Description: dark metallic blue to green back; silver sides and belly; small dark spots on back, sides, and upper half of tail; inside of mouth is gray; breeding adults gray to green on head with red-maroon on sides; males develop kype (hooked snout)

Similar Species: Chinook Salmon (pg. 102), Pink Salmon (pg. 106), Rainbow Trout (pg. 100)

Coho Salmon   **Chinook Salmon**   **Pink Salmon**

spots only in top half of tail   small spots throughout tail   eye-size spots throughout tail

Coho Salmon   **Rainbow Trout**

inside of mouth is gray   inside of mouth is white

COHO SALMON
Oncorhynchus kisutch

Other Names: silver salmon, sea trout, blueback

Habitat: open ocean near clear, gravel-bottomed spawning streams; within 10 miles of shore on the Great Lakes

Range: the Pacific Ocean north from California to Japan; the Atlantic Coast of the U.S.; the Great Lakes; Minnesota—Lake Superior, and North Shore tributary streams during spawning

Food: smelt, alewives, and other fish

Reproduction: spawns in October and November; adults migrate up tributary streams to build nests on gravel bars; parent fish die shortly after spawning

Record and Average Size: Minnesota state record—10 lb., 6.5 oz., 27.3 in.; Average Size—3 to 5 lb. and 14 to 20 in.

Fishing ⬤ Tip: In late fall, fishing gold spoons from Lake Superior breakwalls can be productive.

Notes: A very strong fighter and excellent table fare, the Coho was stocked in the Great Lakes by the Michigan DNR in 1965 and by Minnesota in the late '60s. Minnesota's stocking was not as successful and has been discontinued. There is little natural reproduction in North Shore streams due to the cold-water temperatures and waterfalls that block migration to suitable spawning beds. However, reproduction in other areas of the lake helps support a popular fishery here. With an average summer harvest of 3,200 fish, the Coho is second only to Lake Trout in terms of angler catches on Minnesota's portion of Lake Superior, according to the DNR's annual creel survey.

Description: steel-blue to blue-green back with silver sides; dark spots on back and tail, some as large as the eye; breeding males develop a large hump in front of the dorsal fin and a hooked upper jaw (kype); both sexes are pink during spawn

Similar Species: Chinook Salmon (pg. 102), Coho Salmon (pg. 104), Brown Trout (pg. 96), Rainbow Trout (pg. 100)

Pink Salmon

eye-size spots throughout tail

Chinook Salmon

small spots throughout tail

Coho Salmon

spots only in top half of tail

Pink Salmon

dark tongue and jaw tip

Coho Salmon

inside of mouth is gray

Brown Trout

inside of mouth is white

Rainbow Trout

inside of mouth is white

PINK SALMON
Oncorhynchus gorbuscha

Other Names: humpback salmon, humpy, autumn salmon

Habitat: coastal Pacific Ocean and open water of the Great Lakes; spawns in clear streams

Range: coastal Pacific Ocean from northern California to Alaska; introduced to Great Lakes; Minnesota— Lake Superior

Food: small fish, crustaceans

Reproduction: spawns in fall in tributary streams, usually at two years of age; female builds nest on gravel bar, then covers fertilized eggs; adults die after spawning

Record and Average Size: Minnesota state record—4 lb., 8 oz., 23.5 in.; Average Size—1 to 2 lb. and 14 to 18 in.

Fishing ⬭ Tip: Small, bright, active lures may entice non-feeding spawners to strike.

Notes: This Pacific salmon was unintentionally released into Thunder Bay in 1956 and has since spread throughout the Great Lakes. It spends 2 to 3 years in the open lake, then moves into streams to spawn and die. Often seen along the lakeshore during the odd-year spawning run; it is less common in even years. Pink Salmon are not often caught by anglers and are not considered great table fare; the flesh deteriorates rapidly and must be quickly put on ice.

Description: sides silver with faint pink or purple tinge; dark back; light-colored tail; small mouth; long body but deeper than Rainbow Smelt

Similar Species: Lake Whitefish (pg. 110); Mooneye (pg. 76), Rainbow Smelt (pg. 116)

Cisco
jaws equal length or slight underbite

Lake Whitefish
snout protrudes beyond lower jaw

Cisco
adipose fin

Mooneye
lacks adipose fin

Cisco
deep body, inconspicuous teeth

Rainbow Smelt
slim body, prominent teeth

CISCO
Coregonus artedi

Salmonidae

Other Names: shallow water, common or Great Lakes cisco; lake herring, tullibee

Habitat: shoal waters of the Great Lakes and nutrient-poor inland lakes with oxygen-rich depths that remain cool during the summer

Range: northeastern U.S., Great Lakes, and Canada; Minnesota—Lake Superior and some deep inland lakes

Food: plankton, small crustaceans, aquatic insects

Reproduction: spawns in November and December when water temperatures reach the lower 30s; eggs are deposited over clean bottoms, usually in 3 to 8 feet of water

Record and Average Size: Minnesota state record— (Tullibee) 5 lb., 13 oz., 20.75 in.; Average Size—12 to 16 oz. and 10 to 14 in.

Fishing ⬭ Tip: Tullibees respond well to tiny spinner baits when mayflies are emerging.

Notes: Ciscoes were once the most productive commercial fish in the Great Lakes and are still common in Lake Superior. The flesh is oily but delicious smoked; many fish marketed as "smoked whitefish" are really Ciscoes. The Cisco's inland form is known as the tullibee and varies in shape from lake to lake. Ten Mile Lake has slender dwarf tullibees; Lake Itasca has deep-bodied 4-pounders.

Description: silver with dark brown to olive back and tail; snout protrudes past lower jaw; mouth is small, with two small flaps between the openings of each nostril

Similar Species: Cisco (pg. 108), Mooneye (pg. 76), Rainbow Smelt (pg. 116)

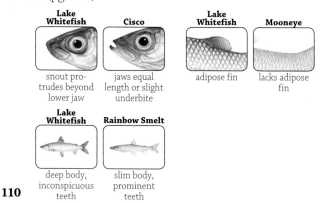

Lake Whitefish	Cisco	Lake Whitefish	Mooneye
snout protrudes beyond lower jaw	jaws equal length or slight underbite	adipose fin	lacks adipose fin

Lake Whitefish	Rainbow Smelt
deep body, inconspicuous teeth	slim body, prominent teeth

LAKE WHITEFISH
Coregonus clupeaformis

Other Names: eastern, common, or Great Lakes whitefish; gizzard fish, Sault whitefish

Habitat: large, deep, clean inland lakes with cool, oxygen-rich depths during the summer; shallow areas of the Great Lakes

Range: from the Great Lakes north across North America; Minnesota—Lake Superior and large inland lakes north of Mille Lacs Lake

Food: zooplankton, insects, small fish

Reproduction: spawns on shallow gravel bars in late fall when water temperatures reach the low 30s; occasionally ascends streams to spawn

Record and Average Size: Minnesota state record—12 lb., 4.5 oz., 28.5 in.; Average Size—2 to 5 lb. and 10 to 18 in.

Fishing ⬤Tip: In inland lakes, Lake Whitefish can be caught fishing small minnows in the deepest parts of the lake.

Notes: The Lake Whitefish is the largest whitefish in North America; it was a significant part of Minnesota's commercial fishery until the mid-1950s, when populations began to decline (though scientists aren't exactly sure why). Just before the ice forms in the fall, Lake Whitefish enter shallows to spawn; spearing/netting was once a popular pastime. A few sportsmen still fish or spear whitefish in the winter and fewer still pull nets under the ice. Along with Walleyes, Lake Whitefish are considered by many to be the finest food fish from Minnesota waters.

111

Description: blotchy brown coloration; large mouth; eyes set almost on top of the broad head; large, wing-like pectoral fins; lacks scales

Similar Species: Round Goby (pg. 50)

Mottled Sculpin

lacks scales

Round Goby

scales on body

MOTTLED SCULPIN
Cottus bairdii

Other Names: common sculpin, muddler, or gudgeon

Habitat: cool, mineral-rich streams and clear lakes; favors areas with rocks or vegetation

Range: the eastern U.S. through Canada to the Hudson Bay and the Rocky Mountains; Minnesota—statewide

Food: aquatic invertebrates, fish eggs, small fish

Reproduction: spawns in April and May in water that's 63–74 degrees; male fans out a cavity beneath a rock, ledge, or log and attracts females via vigorous courtship displays; spawning fish turn upside down and deposit eggs on underside of nest cover; male guards and cleans the eggs after spawning

Record and Average Size: Minnesota state record—none; Average Size—4 to 5 in.

Fishing 🎣 Tip: Sculpins could be used for bait but are hard to collect.

Notes: The Mottled Sculpin is the most common sculpin in Minnesota. One of four sculpin species (the others are the Fourhorn, Slimy, and Spoonhead), it can be found in many cool streams and in some clear northern lakes. Though scary-looking, it is harmless and a food source for a variety of predators. Sculpins can modify their body color to blend in with the surroundings. These closely related sculpins of Lake Superior are important forage fish for Lake Trout. The Slimy Sculpin inhabits shallow areas and tributary streams, while the Fourhorn and Spoonhead Sculpin occupy deeper water.

113

Description: long, thin body; sides bright silver with conspicuous black stripe; upturned mouth; two dorsal fins

Similar Species: Common Shiner (pg. 72), Rainbow Smelt (pg. 116)

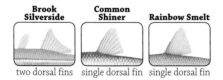

Brook Silverside — two dorsal fins Common Shiner — single dorsal fin Rainbow Smelt — single dorsal fin

BROOK SILVERSIDE
Labidesthes sicculus

Other Names: northern or brook silverside, skipjack, friar

Habitat: surface of clear lakes and large streams

Range: Southeastern U.S. to the Great Lakes; Minnesota—central Minnesota, Mississippi River above St. Anthony Falls

Food: aquatic and flying insects, spiders

Reproduction: spawns in late spring and early summer; eggs are laid in sticky strings that attach to vegetation; adults die soon after spawning

Record and Average Size: Minnesota state record—none; Average Size—2 to 4 in.

Fishing Tip: Silversides are not well suited to use as bait. They are not hardy and tend to jump out of the bait pail.

Notes: The Brook Silverside belongs to a large family of fish that is mostly tropical or subtropical and primarily found in salt water. It is a flashy fish often seen cruising near the surface in small schools. Its upturned mouth is an adaptation to surface feeding. It is not uncommon to see a Brook Silverside leap from the water, flying fish-style, in pursuit of prey. Because of this tendency to jump, coupled with a lack of hardiness when kept in captivity, it is a poor aquarium fish, despite its beauty.

Description: large mouth with prominent teeth; jaw extends to rear margin of the eye; dark green back; violet-blue sides and white belly; deeply forked tail; adipose fin

Similar Species: Cisco (pg. 108), Lake Whitefish (pg. 110), Common Shiner (pg. 72), Brook Silverside (pg. 114)

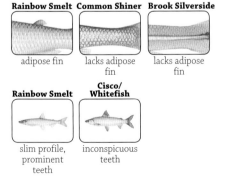

Rainbow Smelt
adipose fin

Common Shiner
lacks adipose fin

Brook Silverside
lacks adipose fin

Rainbow Smelt
slim profile, prominent teeth

Cisco/ Whitefish
inconspicuous teeth

RAINBOW SMELT
Osmerus mordax

Osmeridae

Other Names: ice or frost fish, lake herring, leefish

Habitat: open oceans and large lakes; tributaries at spawning

Range: coastal Pacific, Atlantic and Arctic Oceans; landlocked in northeastern U.S. and southeastern Canada; Minnesota— Lake Superior and a few lakes in Pine and Cook counties

Food: crustaceans, insect larvae, small fish

Reproduction: spawning takes place in May, at night, in the first mile of tributary streams

Record and Average Size: Minnesota state record—none; Average Size—5 to 10 in.

Fishing ⬤ Tip: Smelt are good Lake Trout bait; fish them near the bottom in early spring.

Notes: A saltwater fish that enters fresh water to spawn, the Rainbow Smelt was introduced into some of the Great Lakes in 1912 to support salmon stocks. Smelt made it to Lake Superior in 1930. This small fish flourished and was soon making spectacular spawning runs along Minnesota's North Shore. With the introduction of salmon and the recovery of Lake Trout, the smelt population crashed in the 1980s and has not fully recovered.

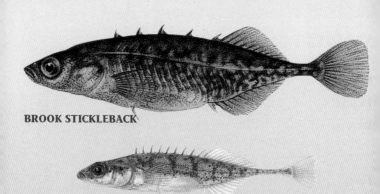

BROOK STICKLEBACK

NINESPINE STICKLEBACK

Description: both Brook and Ninespine Sticklebacks are brown with torpedo-shaped bodies and a very narrow caudal peduncle (the area just before the tail); the front portion of dorsal fin has short, separated spines; pelvic fins are abdominal and reduced to a single spine; small, sharp teeth

Similar Species: Brook Stickleback, Ninespine Stickleback

Brook Stickleback

4 to 6 dorsal spines (usually 5)

Ninespine Stickleback

8 to 11 dorsal spines (usually 9)

STICKLEBACKS

Culaea inconstans, Pungitius pungitius

Gasterosteidae

Other Names: common stickleback, spiny minnow

Habitat: shallows of cool streams and lakes

Range: Kansas through the northern U.S. and Canada; Minnesota—Brook Stickleback, statewide, Ninespine Stickleback, Lake Superior and the Rainy River

Food: small aquatic animals, occasionally algae

Reproduction: when water reaches 50–68 degrees, the male builds a golf ball-size, globular nest of sticks, algae, and other plant matter on submerged vegetation; females deposit eggs and depart, often plowing a hole in the side of the nest in the process; the male repairs any damage and viciously guards the eggs until hatching; an ambitious male may build a second, larger nest and transfer the eggs

Record and Average Size: Minnesota state record—none; Average Size—1 to 3 in.

Fishing ⬤ Tip: Sticklebacks are often found mixed in with crappie minnows and are discarded by anglers, but they are fine as bait.

Notes: Most members of the stickleback family are marine fish, but some are equally at home in fresh or salt water. The Brook Stickleback is Minnesota's most common stickleback and can be found in most streams and lakes. The Ninespine Stickleback is restricted to Lake Superior and the Rainy River. These pugnacious little predators make fun aquarium fish and will readily build and defend nests in captivity.

119

Description: slate gray to brown sides, white belly; bony plates on skin; tail lacks plates and is shark-like with upper lobe longer than lower; blunt snout with four barbels; spiracles (openings between eye and corner of gill)

Similar Species: Shovelnose Sturgeon (pg. 122)

Lake Sturgeon

spiracle between eye and gill

Shovelnose Sturgeon

lacks spiracles

LAKE STURGEON
Acipenser fulvescens

Acipenseridae

Other Names: rock sturgeon, smoothback

Habitat: quiet waters of large rivers and lakes

Range: Hudson Bay, the Great Lakes, the Mississippi and Missouri River drainages southeast to Alabama; Minnesota—the Mississippi (below St. Anthony Falls), St. Croix, Rainy and Red River drainages; Lake Superior and some Canadian border lakes

Food: snails, clams, crayfish, aquatic insects

Reproduction: spawns in April through June in lake shallows and tributary streams; a single female may produce up to 1 million eggs

Record and Average Size: Minnesota state record—94 lb., 4 oz., 70 in.; Average Size—10 to 30 lb. and 20 to 40 in.

Fishing ⬭ Tip: Large grayfish tails are good sturgeon bait.

Notes: Minnesota's largest fish, Lake Sturgeon once exceeded 100 pounds, with one historic Lake Superior specimen reputedly weighing it at more than 300 pounds. Today, due to commercial fishing, dams, habitat alteration, and pollution, this slow-growing fish averages 5 to 40 pounds and is relatively rare except in select waters where some recreational fisheries still exist. Thanks to a regulated harvest, cleaner water, and improved access to habitat, sturgeon are slowly increasing in numbers. A 78-inch Lake Sturgeon caught in the St. Croix River in February 2019 was estimated to weigh 120 pounds; it is likely the largest fish ever caught in the state.

121

Description: coppery, dark tan or light brown back and sides; light belly; long, flat snout; shovel-shaped head; bony plates instead of scales; shark-like tail with upper lobe ending in a long filament

Similar Species: Lake Sturgeon (pg. 120)

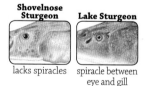

Shovelnose Sturgeon — lacks spiracles

Lake Sturgeon — spiracle between eye and gill

SHOVELNOSE STURGEON
Scaphirhynchus platorynchus

Acipenseridae

Other Names: hackleback, sand sturgeon, switchtail

Habitat: open, flowing channels of rivers and large streams, typically with sand or gravel bottom

Range: Hudson Bay south through central U.S., west to New Mexico and east to Kentucky; Minnesota—the lower Mississippi, St. Croix, and Minnesota Rivers and larger tributary streams

Food: clams, snails, crayfish, aquatic insects

Reproduction: spawns in May and June in water temperatures of 65–71 degrees; adults migrate upriver or into small tributaries to spawn over gravel or rocks in swift current

Record and Average Size: Minnesota state record—5 lb., 4 oz., 34 in.; Average Size—2 to 3 lb. and 18 to 24 in.

Fishing Tip: Fish grayfish tails, or worms, on the bottom in deep channels.

Notes: The Shovelnose Sturgeon is the smallest sturgeon in North America. Sturgeon belong to a prehistoric-looking family of fish with cartilage instead of bones and hard plates in place of scales. Like the Lake Sturgeon, it suctions up food off the bottom. Once netted commercially in Minnesota for both meat and caviar, it is now uncommon in most waters, largely due to a loss of spawning and nursery habitat.

123

Description: olive-brown to bronze back; sides dull olive fading to white belly; blunt snout; rounded head; long dorsal fin; upper lip even with lower margin of eye

Similar Species: Common Carp (pg. 62), Black Buffalo (pg. 126), Smallmouth Buffalo (pg. 128)

Bigmouth Buffalo

upper lip level with lower edge of eye

Black Buffalo

upper lip well below eye

Smallmouth Buffalo

upper lip well below eye

Bigmouth Buffalo

forward-facing mouth, lacks barbels

Common Carp

downturned mouth with barbels

BIGMOUTH BUFFALO
Ictiobus cyprinellus

Other Names: baldpate, blue router, mongrel, round buffalo

Habitat: soft-bottomed shallows of large lakes, sloughs, and oxbows; slow-flowing streams and rivers

Range: Saskatchewan to Lake Erie south through the Mississippi River drainage to the Gulf of Mexico; Minnesota—the Red, Minnesota, St. Croix, and Mississippi River drainages

Food: small mollusks, insect larvae, zooplankton

Reproduction: makes spectacular spawning runs in clear, shallow water of flooded fields and marshes during April and May; spawns when water temperatures reach the low 60s

Record and Average Size: Minnesota state record—41 lb., 11 oz., 38.5 in.; Average Size—10 to 15 lb. and 18 to 24 in.

Fishing ⬤ Tip: Buffalo are filter feeders that are hard to hook but can be caught by floating small pieces of nightcrawlers in slow backwater currents.

Notes: The Bigmouth Buffalo is a schooling, big-water fish that inhabits the large, shallow lakes and streams in the less-forested parts of Minnesota. Commercially harvested in Lake St. Croix in the summer and the lower Mississippi River in the winter. This largest of the Minnesota suckers can withstand low oxygen levels, high water temperatures, and some turbidity but prefers clear, clean water for foraging.

Description: slate green to dark gray back; sides have a blue-bronze sheen; deep body with a sloping back that supports a long dorsal fin; upper lip well below eye

Similar Species: Bigmouth Buffalo (pg. 124), Smallmouth Buffalo (pg. 128), Common Carp (pg. 62)

Black Buffalo	**Bigmouth Buffalo**	**Smallmouth Buffalo**
upper lip well below eye	upper lip level with lower edge of eye	upper lip well below eye

Black Buffalo	**Common Carp**
mouth lacks barbels	barbels below mouth

BLACK BUFFALO

Ictiobus niger

Other Names: buoy tender; current or deepwater buffalo

Habitat: deep, fast water of large streams; deep sloughs, backwaters and impoundments

Range: the lower Great Lakes and the Mississippi River drainage west to South Dakota, south to New Mexico and Louisiana; Minnesota—the lower Mississippi and Minnesota Rivers

Food: aquatic insects, crustaceans, algae

Reproduction: spawning takes place in April and May; fish move up tributaries to lay eggs in flooded sloughs and marshes

Record and Average Size: Minnesota state record—20 lb., 5 oz., 34.2 in.; Average size—8 to 10 lb. and 15 to 20 in.

Fishing ⬤ Tip: Fish the mouth of tributary streams with small baits during the spawning run.

Notes: The Black Buffalo is a southern species that is very uncommon in the Minnesota and Mississippi Rivers. They inhabit the deep, strong currents of large rivers (hence the nickname "current buffalo"). It is rarely caught on hook and line, but it's notable because of its size and strong fight. Black Buffalo can hybridize with Smallmouth Buffalo.

Description: slate-green back with bronze sides; large, dark eye; deep, laterally compressed body; rounded head; blunt snout; small, downturned mouth with thick lips

Similar Species: Common Carp (pg. 62), Bigmouth Buffalo (pg. 124), Black Buffalo (pg. 126)

Smallmouth Buffalo

upper lip well below eye

Bigmouth Buffalo

upper lip level with eye

Smallmouth Buffalo

mouth lacks barbels

Common Carp

barbels below mouth

Smallmouth Buffalo

back steeply arched with pronounced hump

Black Buffalo

rounded back without hump

SMALLMOUTH BUFFALO

Ictiobus bubalus

Other Names: razorback, highback, humpback, or thick-lipped buffalo

Habitat: moderate to swift currents in the deep, clean water of larger streams and lakes

Range: the Missouri, Mississippi, and Ohio River drainages south to the Gulf of Mexico and west into New Mexico; Minnesota—the St. Croix River below St. Anthony Falls; the lower Mississippi and Minnesota Rivers

Food: insect larvae, small crustaceans

Reproduction: spawns in flooded fields and marshes in early summer when water temperatures reach the low 60s

Record and Average Size: Minnesota state Record—20 lb., 32 in.; Average size—5 to 10 lb. and 15 to 24 in.

Fishing ⬭ Tip: Drift small, prepared baits or insects in the mouth of tributary streams.

Notes: This smaller cousin of the Bigmouth Buffalo requires deeper, cleaner water and feeds more heavily on aquatic insect larvae. The Smallmouth Buffalo is commercially harvested, many of them being shipped live to markets on the coast.

Description: bright silver, often with a yellow tinge; fins clear; deep body with a round, blunt head; leading rays of dorsal fin extend into a large, arching "quill"

Similar Species: Common Carp (pg. 62), Smallmouth Buffalo (pg. 128)

Quillback

mouth lacks barbels

Common Carp

barbels below mouth

Quillback

longest dorsal ray similar to length of base

Smallmouth Buffalo

longest dorsal ray much shorter than base

QUILLBACK
Carpiodes cyprinus

Other Names: silver carp, carpsucker, lake quillback

Habitat: slow-flowing streams and rivers; backwaters and lakes, particularly areas with soft bottoms

Range: south-central Canada through the Great Lakes to the eastern U.S., south through the Mississippi River drainage to the Gulf; Minnesota—statewide except the Upper Mississippi River and Lake Superior drainages

Food: insects, plant matter, decaying material on bottom

Reproduction: ascends tributaries from late spring through early summer; spawns over sand, gravel, or mud

Record and Average Size: Minnesota state record—7 lb., 4 oz., 22.6 in.; Average Size—1 to 3 lb. and 10 to 15 in.

Fishing ⬭ Tip: In clear streams, drift small pieces of nightcrawlers into the pools below riffles.

Notes: The Quillback is one of four North American fish known as carpsuckers. Three carpsuckers are found in Minnesota, but the species are not easy to differentiate. Quillbacks are a common fish throughout most of Minnesota. They are a bottom-feeding, schooling fish with little importance to anglers, though the fillets are reportedly of good flavor. Historically, Quillbacks were part of the commercial harvest in Red Lake and the Mississippi River.

Description: olive-brown to brownish back; sides silver to bronze; white belly; bright red tail; blunt nose; sickle-shaped dorsal fin

Similar Species: Longnose Sucker (pg. 134), White Sucker (pg. 136)

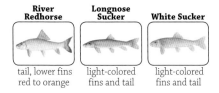

River Redhorse	Longnose Sucker	White Sucker
tail, lower fins red to orange	light-colored fins and tail	light-colored fins and tail

RIVER REDHORSE
Moxostoma carinatum

Catostomidae

Other Names: redhorse, redfin sucker

Habitat: clean streams and rivers with sand, gravel, or rocky bottom; occasionally in clear lakes

Range: the Great Lakes states to New England south to the Gulf; Minnesota—statewide

Food: insects, crustaceans, mussels, plant debris

Reproduction: spawns from late May to June in small tributary streams; the male builds a 4- to 8-foot-diameter nest on gravel shoals, then courts females by darting back and forth across the nest; a second male may join the display and spawning process

Record and Average Size: Minnesota state record—12 lb., 10 oz., 28.4 in.; Average Size—2 to 6 lb. and 12 to 18 in.

Fishing ⬤Tip: Fish wet flies or worms in rocky, fast water.

Notes: The River Redhorse is the most common of the six redhorse species found in Minnesota. It can be distinguished from the others by its bright red tail. All redhorses are clean-water fish and are very susceptible to increased turbidity and pollutants. They all fight well on light tackle and are good when smoked.

Description: black, brown, to dark olive back; slate to pale brown sides fading to white belly; males develop a red band during breeding; long snout protruding beyond upper lip

Similar Species: River Redhorse (pg. 132), White Sucker (pg. 136)

Longnose Sucker

White Sucker

Longnose Sucker

River Redhorse

snout extends well beyond upper lip

snout barely extends past upper lip

fins white to yellowish

fins red to orange

LONGNOSE SUCKER
Catostomus catostomus

Other Names: sturgeon, red, or redside sucker

Habitat: primarily shallow waters of large, cold lakes and streams, occasionally in deep water

Range: Siberia across Canada through Great Lakes to the eastern U.S.; Missouri and Columbia River systems in the West; Minnesota—Lake Superior, Lake Vermilion, and Lake of the Woods; Rainy River and its tributaries

Food: small crustaceans, plant material

Reproduction: spawns in April and May, when fish crowd small tributaries

Record and Average Size: Minnesota state record—3 lb., 10 oz., 21 in.; Average Size—1 to 2 lb. and 10 to 16 in.

Fishing ⬤ Tip: Try drifting yellow trout PowerBait among the rocks in river eddies.

Notes: This is a northern coldwater fish found in both the Old World and the New World. Though primarily known as a shallow-water fish, it has been taken as deep as 600 feet in Lake Superior. Large numbers of Longnose Suckers crowd some North Shore streams during the spawning run. The Longnose Sucker is delicious when smoked, and smoked fish connoisseurs argue that it is superior to the White Sucker in flavor.

Description: back olive to brown; sides gray to silver; belly white; gray dorsal fin and tail; other fins clear or whitish; rounded head; blunt snout

Similar Species: Longnose Sucker (pg. 134), River Redhorse (pg. 132)

White Sucker	Longnose Sucker	White Sucker	River Redhorse
snout barely extends past upper lip	snout extends well beyond upper lip	light-colored lower fins	fins red to orange

WHITE SUCKER
Catostomus commersonii

Other Names: common, coarse-scaled, or eastern sucker; black mullet

Habitat: clean lakes and streams with some rock or gravel areas for spawning

Range: Canada through central and eastern U.S. south to a line from New Mexico to South Carolina; Minnesota—statewide

Food: insects, crustaceans, plant matter

Reproduction: spawns over gravel or coarse sand in April and early May; adults migrate up small tributaries; in large lakes, spawning may occur along shoreline shallows

Record and Average Size: Minnesota state record—9 lb., 1 oz., 24.25 in.; 1 to 3 lb. and 12 to 18 in.

Fishing ⬭Tip: In early spring, fish with worms at the mouth of small streams.

Notes: The White Sucker is probably the most common fish in Minnesota and one of the most important statewide. Highly productive, it provides a large source of forage for game fish and is a mainstay in the live bait industry. A few folks pursue White Suckers during the spring spawning run with spears or dip nets. White Sucker meat is bony but delectable when smoked or used in soups and chowders.

Description: dark green back, greenish sides often with dark lateral band; belly white to gray; large, forward-facing mouth; lower jaw extends to rear margin of eye

Similar Species: Smallmouth Bass (pg. 140)

mouth extends beyond dark orange eye

mouth does not extend beyond red eye

LARGEMOUTH BASS
Micropterus salmoides

Other Names: black bass, green bass, green trout, slough bass

Habitat: shallow, fertile, weedy lakes and river backwaters

Range: southern Canada through U.S. into Mexico; widely introduced worldwide; Minnesota—statewide, rare in the northeast and Lake Superior drainage

Food: small fish, frogs, crayfish, insects, leeches

Reproduction: in May and June, when water temperatures reach 60 degrees, male builds nest in 2–8 feet of water, usually on firm bottom in weedy cover; male guards eggs and fry until the "brood swarm" disperses

Record and Average Size: Minnesota state record: 8 lb., 15 oz., 23.5 in.; Average Size—1 to 3 lb. and 10 to 20 in.

Fishing ⬤ Tip: Retrieving lures very slowly is often the most productive approach for bass.

Notes: The Largemouth Bass is the largest member of the sunfish family in Minnesota. Of the two recognized subspecies, only the "northern strain" of the species (*Micropterus salmoides salmoides)* exists in the state. The most sought-after game fish in North America, it is known for spirited battles and acrobatic leaps. The Largemouth Bass will devour any live prey that fits in its mouth.

Description: back and sides mottled dark green to bronze or pale gold, often with dark vertical bands; white belly; stout body; large, forward-facing mouth; red eye

Similar Species: Largemouth Bass (pg. 138)

Smallmouth Bass

mouth does not extend beyond red eye

Largemouth Bass

mouth extends beyond dark orange eye

SMALLMOUTH BASS
Micropterus dolomieu

Other Names: bronzeback, brown or redeye bass, redeye, white or mountain trout

Habitat: clear, swift-flowing streams and rivers; clear lakes with gravel or rocky shorelines

Range: extensively introduced throughout North America; Minnesota—statewide

Food: small fish, crayfish, insects, frogs

Reproduction: in May and June, when the water temperature reaches the mid to high 60s, the male sweeps out a nest in a gravel bed, typically in 3–10 feet of water; nest is often next to a log or boulder; male guards nest and young until fry disperse

Record and Average Size: Minnesota state record—8 lb.; Average Size—1 to 3 lb. and 10 to 20 in.

Fishing ⬤ Tip: Fish imitation-crayfish lures in the shade of large rocks or brush.

Notes: Revered by anglers as a world-class game fish, the Smallmouth Bass is noted for powerful fights and wild jumps. Avoiding weedbeds, it prefers deeper, more open water than Largemouth Bass. Though the range of this slow-maturing fish has expanded, its numbers are decreasing in some areas due to overfishing and habitat loss. Still, many Minnesota lakes and rivers offer high-quality bass fishing and some, like Mille Lacs and Rainy Lakes, are legendary.

Description: black to dark-olive back; silver sides with dark green or black blotches; its back is more arched and the depression above the eye is more pronounced than in the White Crappie

Similar Species: White Crappie (pg. 144)

Black Crappie	White Crappie		Black Crappie	White Crappie

| usually 7 to 8 spines in dorsal fin | usually 5 to 6 spines in dorsal fin | | dorsal fin length equal to distance from eye to dorsal | dorsal fin shorter than distance from eye to dorsal |

BLACK CRAPPIE
Pomoxis nigromaculatus

Other Names: papermouth, speck, speckled perch

Habitat: quiet, clear water of streams and midsize lakes; often associated with vegetation but also roams deep, open basins and flats, particularly during winter

Range: southern Manitoba through the Atlantic and southeastern states; introduced in the West; Minnesota—statewide, less common in northeast

Food: small fish, aquatic insects, zooplankton

Reproduction: spawns in shallow weedbeds from May to June when water temperatures reach the high 50s; male sweeps out a circular nest, typically on fine gravel or sand; male guards the nest and fry; may spawn in colonies

Record and Average Size: Minnesota state record—5 lb., 21 in.; Average Size—6 to 16 oz. and 8 to 10 in.

Fishing ⬤ Tip: Try flies under a split shot when the bite is slow.

Notes: Pursued year-round by Minnesota anglers for its sweet-tasting white fillets, it is an aggressive carnivore that will hit everything from waxworms and minnows to jigging spoons and small crankbaits. Actively feeds at night and often suspends well off the bottom in pursuit of plankton and baitfish. Requires clearer water and more vegetation than White Crappie.

Description: greenish back; silvery green to white sides with 7 to 9 dark vertical bars; the only sunfish with 5 or 6 spines in both the dorsal and anal fin

Similar Species: Black Crappie (pg. 142)

White Crappie	**Black Crappie**	**White Crappie**	**Black Crappie**
usually 5 to 6 spines in dorsal fin	usually 7 to 8 spines in dorsal fin	dorsal fin shorter than distance from eye to dorsal	dorsal fin length equal to distance from eye to dorsal

WHITE CRAPPIE
Pomoxis annularis

Other Names: silver, pale, or ringed crappie; papermouth

Habitat: slightly silty streams and midsize to large lakes; prefers less vegetation than the Black Crappie

Range: North Dakota south and east to the Gulf and Atlantic states except peninsular Florida; Minnesota—statewide, less common in northeast

Food: aquatic insects, small fish, plankton

Reproduction: spawns on firm sand or gravel when the water temperature approaches 60 degrees; male builds a shallow, round nest and guards eggs and young after spawning

Record and Average Size: Minnesota state record—3 lb., 15 oz., 18 in.; Average Size—5 to 14 oz. and 6 to 9 in.

Fishing ⬭ Tip: In midsummer, slowly troll minnows far behind the boat to locate schools.

Notes: Less common in Minnesota than the Black Crappie but may be increasing in abundance with the increased siltation of streams and lakes. Where Black and White Crappies are found together, they will hybridize. White Crappies are often found in large schools suspended off the bottom and away from weeds or structure. Actively feeds at night and during the winter.

Description: dark olive to green on back, blending to silver-gray, copper, orange, purple, or brown on sides; 5 to 9 dark vertical bars on sides that fade with age; yellow belly and copper breast; large dark gill spot that extends completely to gill margin; dark spot on rear margin of dorsal fin

Similar Species: Green Sunfish (pg. 148), Pumpkinseed (pg. 152)

Bluegill
small mouth

Green Sunfish
large mouth

Bluegill
dark gill spot

Pumpkinseed
orange crescent

Bluegill
dark spot on dorsal fin

Pumpkinseed
no dark spot

BLUEGILL
Lepomis macrochirus

Other Names: 'gill, bull, bream, copperbelly

Habitat: medium to large streams, and most lakes with weedy bays or shorelines

Range: Southern Canada into Mexico; Minnesota—statewide except the northeast

Food: insects, small fish, leeches, snails, zooplankton, algae

Reproduction: spawns from late May to early August; male excavates nest in gravel or coarse sand, often in shallow weeds, in colonies of up to 50 nests; often, a smaller "cuckholder" male darts into the nest and fertilizes eggs; male guards nest until fry disperse

Record and Average Size: Minnesota state record—2 lb., 13 oz.; Average Size—5 to 10 oz. and 6 to 10 inches

Fishing Tip: Adding a kernel of corn to your bait will sometimes entice large Bluegills in schools of small ones.

Notes: A favorite of anglers young and old for its tenacious fight and excellent table quality. Small fish are easy to catch near docks in summer. Larger "bulls" favor deep weedbeds close to open water. Bluegills frequently hybridize with other sunfish. All the sunfish have acute daytime vision for feeding on small prey items but see poorly in low light.

Description: dark green back; dark-olive to bluish sides; yellow to cream belly; scales flecked with yellow, producing a brassy appearance; dark gill spot with pale margin; large mouth with thick lips

Similar Species: Bluegill (pg. 146)

Green Sunfish

large mouth

Bluegill

small mouth

GREEN SUNFISH
Lepomis cyanellus

Other Names: green perch, blue-spotted sunfish, sand bass

Habitat: warm, weedy shallow lakes and the backwaters of slow-moving streams

Range: most of the U.S. into Mexico, excluding Florida and the Rocky Mountains; Minnesota—statewide

Food: aquatic insects, crustaceans, small fish

Reproduction: beginning in May and June, male fans out a nest on gravel bottom near weeds or other cover, often in less than 1 foot of water; male may grunt to lure female into nest; after spawning, male guards nest and fry

Record and Average Size: Minnesota state record—1 lb., 4 oz., 10.25 in.; Average Size—4 to 10 oz. and 3 to 7 in.

Fishing ⬭ Tip: At times, green or yellow trout PowerBait is good for sunfish.

Notes: The Green Sunfish is abundant in some lakes yet completely absent from others. It is easy to catch but not a popular sport fish because it rarely reaches more than 5 to 7 inches in length. Very tolerant of high siltation and low oxygen levels, it thrives in warm, weedy lakes and backwaters. It often hybridizes with Bluegill and Pumpkinseed, producing somewhat larger, and more voracious, offspring.

Description: bluish green back fading to orange; about 30 orange or red spots on sides of males, brown spots on females; orange pelvic and anal fins; black gill spot has light margin

Similar Species: Bluegill (pg. 146), Green Sunfish (pg. 148), Pumpkinseed (pg. 152)

Orangespotted Sunfish

light margin on gill spot

Bluegill

gill spot lacks light margin

Pumpkinseed

orange or red crescent on gill

Orangespotted Sunfish

hard spines longer than soft rays

Green Sunfish

hard spines shorter than soft rays

ORANGESPOTTED SUNFISH
Lepomis humilis

Centrarchidae

Other Names: orangespot, dwarf sunfish, pygmy sunfish

Habitat: open to moderately weedy pools in lakes and streams, prefers soft bottoms

Range: Southern Great Lakes through Mississippi River basin to Gulf states; Minnesota—Mississippi River drainage south of Twin Cities; common in Minnesota River tributaries

Food: insects, small crustaceans

Reproduction: male builds and guards nest in shallow water when water temperatures reach mid 60s; colonial nesters

Record and Average Size: Minnesota state record—none; Average Size—3 to 4 oz. and 3 to 4 in.

Fishing ⬭ Tip: A feisty little fish, it'll even bite small, shiny bare hooks.

Notes: This brightly colored sunfish is very common in some lakes, and although it is often caught, it is too small to be a significant panfish. It does, however, make a colorful aquarium pet. The Orangespotted Sunfish is important as a forage species for other game fish and may be important for mosquito larvae control in some areas. It survives well in silty water and tolerates some pollution, making it well suited for small lakes in agricultural areas.

Description: back brown to olive; sides speckled with orange, yellow, blue, and green spots with 7 to 10 vertical bands; chest and belly yellow or orange; black gill spot has light margin with orange or red crescent

Similar Species: Bluegill (pg. 146), Green Sunfish (pg. 148), Orangespotted Sunfish (pg. 150)

Pumpkinseed	**Bluegill**	**Orangespotted Sunfish**
orange or red crescent on gill flap	gill spot lacks light margin	light margin on gill spot

Pumpkinseed	**Green Sunfish**
long, pointed pectoral fin	rounded pectoral fin

PUMPKINSEED
Lepomis gibbosus

Other Names: 'seed, punky, yellow, or round sunfish; bream

Habitat: weedy ponds, clear lakes, slow-moving streams; prefers slightly cooler water than Bluegill

Range: native to eastern and central North America, widely introduced elsewhere; Minnesota—statewide

Food: insects, snails, fish, leeches, small amounts of vegetation

Reproduction: when water temperatures reach 55 to 63 degrees, the male builds nest in gravel among weeds in less than 2 feet of water; nests are located in colonies, often with other sunfish species; male aggressively guards the nest; multiple broods per year are common

Record and Average Size: Minnesota state record—1 lb., 5 oz., 10 in.; Average Size—6 to 10 oz. and 5 to 10 in.

Fishing ⬬Tip: Waxworms are good Pumpkinseed bait, both in summer and winter.

Notes: The Pumpkinseed is one of the most beautiful fish in Minnesota. It often schools under submerged logs or deadfalls and around docks. It is easy to catch on small natural and artificial baits and makes fine table fare. Larger specimens often feed along edges of deep weedbeds during the day and settle to the bottom at night. Hybridization with other sunfish is common. In small lakes, Pumpkinseeds are known for stunting, filling a lake with small individuals and few larger fish; when this happens, the populations of other fish in the lake appear normal.

Description: brown to olive-green back and sides with dark spots and overall bronze appearance; red eye; thicker, heavier body than other sunfish; large mouth

Similar Species: Bluegill (pg. 146), Green Sunfish (pg. 148), Pumpkinseed (pg. 152), Warmouth (pg. 156)

Rock Bass	**Green Sunfish**	**Pumpkinseed**	**Warmouth**
solid dark gill spot	light margin on gill spot	orange or red crescent on gill flap	dark gill spot with light margin

Rock Bass	**Bluegill**
large mouth extends to eye	small mouth does not extend to eye

ROCK BASS
Ambloplites rupestris

Other Names: redeye, goggle eye, rock sunfish

Habitat: vegetation on firm to rocky bottom in clear lakes and medium-size streams

Range: Southern Canada through the central and eastern U.S. to the northern edge of Gulf states; Minnesota—statewide

Food: prefers crayfish, but eats aquatic insects and small fish

Reproduction: when water temperatures reach the high 60s to 70s, the male fans out a coarse gravel nest in weeds and in water less than 3 feet deep; male guards eggs and fry

Record and Average Size: Minnesota state record—2 lb., 13.5 in.; Average Size—8 to 16 oz. and 6 to 10 in.

Fishing ⬤ Tip: Fish small dark green or brown hair jigs on the bottom near weedy rock piles.

Notes: Rock Bass are common in clear northern lakes, where they frequent weedbeds associated with rocks. Though the Rock Bass is plentiful, hard-fighting, and good-tasting, it is seldom targeted by anglers, but it is a willing biter and fun to catch on light tackle. The Rock Bass is often found in schools, which do not stray far from their home territories.

Description: back and sides greenish gray to brown; lightly mottled with faint vertical bands; stout body; large mouth; red eye; 3 to 5 reddish-brown streaks radiate from eye

Similar Species: Bluegill (pg. 146), Green Sunfish (pg. 148), Pumpkinseed (pg. 152), Warmouth (pg. 156)

Warmouth	**Bluegill**	**Green Sunfish**
jaw extends at least to middle of eye	small mouth does not extend to eye	jaw does not extend to middle of eye

Warmouth	**Pumpkinseed**	**Rock Bass**
light margin on gill spot	prominent orange or red crescent on gill spot	dark gill spot lacks light margin

WARMOUTH
Lepomis gulosus

Other Names: goggle-eye, wide-mouth sunfish, stump-knocker, weed bass

Habitat: heavy weeds in turbid lakes, reservoirs, and slow-moving streams

Range: the southern U.S. from Texas to Florida north to the southern Great Lakes region; Minnesota—southeast, mostly in Mississippi River backwaters

Food: small fish, insects, snails, crustaceans

Reproduction: male fans out solitary nest in dense, shallow weeds when the water temperature reaches the low 70s; nest is located by a rock, stump, or weed clump; male guards eggs after spawning

Record and Average Size: Minnesota state record—none; Average Size—8 to 12 oz. and 5 to 8 in.

Fishing ⬤Tip: Fish with small jigs and keep them moving around stumps and logs.

Notes: This secretive sunfish is uncommon in Minnesota. It is a solitary, aggressive sight-feeder, which, when not hiding in dense vegetation, is often found around rocks and submerged stumps. It prefers turbid water and a muddy bottom. It can withstand low oxygen levels, high silt loads, and water temperatures well into the 90s.

Description: bright silver; 6 to 8 distinct, uninterrupted black stripes on each side; front hard-spined portion of dorsal fin separated from soft-rayed rear section; lower jaw protrudes beyond snout

Similar Species: Yellow Bass (pg. 160)

White Bass
lower jaw protrudes beyond snout

Yellow Bass
lower jaw even with snout

White Bass
stripes continuous

Yellow Bass
stripes broken above anal fin

WHITE BASS
Morone chrysops

Other Names: silver bass, streaker, lake bass, sand bass

Habitat: large lakes, rivers, and impoundments with relatively clear water

Range: the Great Lakes region to the Eastern Seaboard, through the southeast to the Gulf, west to Texas; Minnesota—the lower Mississippi, Minnesota, and St. Croix River systems

Food: small fish

Reproduction: spawns in open water over gravel beds or rubble 6–10 feet deep when water temperatures reach 55–70 degrees; a single female may produce more than 500,000 eggs

Record and Average Size: Minnesota state record—4 lb., 8 oz., 20 in.; Average Size—1 to 2 lb. and 8 to 10 in.

Fishing ⬤Tip: In the spring, cast imitation-minnow lures into river eddies.

Notes: Common in big river-lakes, such as Lake St. Croix and Lake Pepin, the White Bass is a willing striker and a hard fighter. Boasting good table quality, its flavor and texture can be improved if the fish is quickly put on ice. It travels in large schools, often near the surface, and can often be spotted by watching for seagulls feeding on frightened baitfish that are fleeing the marauding predators.

159

Description: silvery yellow to brassy sides with yellowish white belly; 6 or 7 black stripes broken above anal fin; forked tail; two sections of dorsal fin connected by membrane

Similar Species: White Bass (pg. 158)

Yellow Bass

lower jaw even with snout

White Bass

jaw protrudes beyond snout

Yellow Bass

stripes broken above anal fin

White Bass

stripes continuous

YELLOW BASS
Morone mississippiensis

Other Names: brassy or gold bass; barfish

Habitat: open water over shallow gravel bars

Range: the Mississippi River drainage south to the Gulf of Mexico; Minnesota—the Mississippi River and its backwaters south of Lake Pepin

Food: small fish, insects, crustaceans

Reproduction: spawns in late spring over gravel bars in the mouths of tributary streams

Record and Average Size: Minnesota state record—none; Average Size—8 to 16 oz. and 6 to 10 in.

Fishing ⬤ Tip: Fish deep backwater sand bars with yellow jigs.

Notes: This close cousin to the White Bass is not very common in Minnesota and is found only in the Mississippi River south of Lake City. Its schooling and feeding habits are similar to those of the White Bass, but it tends to stay in the middle of the water column or near the bottom. The Yellow Bass is a very popular panfish farther south, where its flaky, white flesh is considered superior to that of White Bass.

Description: olive to blackish green back; silver-green sides with no stripes; front spiny dorsal fin connected by a small membrane to the soft-rayed back portion

Similar Species: Yellow Bass (pg. 160), White Bass (pg. 158)

White Perch

no horizontal stripes except on lateral line

White Bass

black horizontal stripes

Yellow Bass

stripes broken above anal fin

WHITE PERCH
Morone americana

Other Names: narrow-mouth bass; silver or sea perch

Habitat: brackish water in coastal areas; nearshore areas of the Great Lakes; expanding range into smaller freshwater lakes and rivers

Range: the central Mississippi River drainage south to the Gulf of Mexico; the Atlantic Coast from Maine to South Carolina; Minnesota—Lake Superior and St. Louis River

Food: fish eggs, minnows, insects, crustaceans

Reproduction: spawns in late spring over gravel bars of tributary streams

Record and Average Size: Minnesota state record—none; Average Size—6 to 16 oz. and 6 to 8 in.

Fishing ⬭Tip: This destructive fish poses a risk to habitats in Minnesota; anglers need to help prevent it from invading other Minnesota habitats.

Notes: The White Perch is a fish native to brackish water in the coastal Atlantic states. White Perch making spawning runs up freshwater tributary streams have become established in some large eastern reservoirs. The White Perch's range is now quickly expanding into many freshwater habitats. They are now common in the Mississippi (south of Minnesota) and Missouri Rivers, and they are expanding into many states. They prey heavily on fish eggs and are detrimental to native species.

Description: overall silvery, almost transparent appearance; mottled brown, tan, or greenish with dark spots on sides; adipose fin; single dorsal fin with two spines and 10 to 11 rays

Similar Species: Yellow Perch (pg. 88), Walleye (pg. 86)

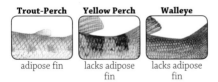

| **Trout-Perch** | **Yellow Perch** | **Walleye** |
| adipose fin | lacks adipose fin | lacks adipose fin |

TROUT-PERCH
Percopsis omiscomaycus

Other Names: grounder, sand minnow

Habitat: prefers clear to slightly turbid (cloudy) water over sand or gravel; avoids soft-bottomed shallows

Range: east-central U.S. through Canada to Alaska; Minnesota—statewide

Food: insects, copepods, small fish

Reproduction: spawns from May to August over sand bars and rocks in lakes and tributary streams

Record and Average Size: Minnesota state record—none; Average Size—3 to 5 in.

Fishing Tip: A good baitfish, but seining for it is only productive in shallow water at night.

Notes: A deepwater fish by day, the Trout-Perch is seldom seen unless it washes up on a beach, where it is often mistaken for a juvenile Walleye. Nocturnal migration patterns bring large schools into the shallows to feed under the cover of darkness. It is an important forage species for Walleyes, Northern Pike, and Lake Trout.

GLOSSARY

adipose fin a small, fleshy fin without rays, located on the midline of the fish's back between the dorsal fin and the tail

air bladder a balloon-like organ located in the gut area of a fish, used to control buoyancy—and in the respiration of some species such as gar; also called "swim bladder" or "gas bladder"

alevin a newly hatched fish that still has its yolk sac

anadromous a fish that hatches in fresh water, migrates to the ocean, then re-enters streams or rivers from the sea (or large inland body of water) to spawn

anal fin a single fin located on the bottom of the fish near the tail

annulus a mark or ring on the scales, spine, vertebrae, or otoliths that scientists use to determine a fish's age

anterior toward the front of a fish, opposite of posterior

bands horizontal marks running lengthwise along the side of a fish

barbel thread-like sensory structures on a fish's head, often near the mouth, commonly called "whiskers"; used for taste or smell

bars vertical markings on the side of a fish

benthic organisms living in or on the bottom

brood swarm a large group or "cloud" of young fish, such as bullheads

cardiform teeth small teeth on the lips of catfish

carnivore a fish that feeds on other fish (also called a piscivore) or animals

catadromous a fish that lives in fresh water and migrates into saltwater to spawn, such as the American Eel

caudal fin the tail or tail fin

caudal peduncle the portion of the fish's body located between the anal fin and the beginning of the tail

coldwater referring to a species or environment; in fish, often a species of trout or salmon found in water that rarely exceeds 70 degrees; also used to describe a lake or river according to average summer temperature

copepod a small (less than 2 mm) crustacean that is part of the zooplankton community

crustacean a crayfish, water flea, crab, or other animal belonging to group of mostly aquatic species that have paired antennae, jointed legs, and an exterior skeleton (exoskeleton); common food for many fish

dorsal relating to the top of the fish, on or near the back; opposite of the ventral, or lower, part of the fish

dorsal fin the fin or fins located along the top of a fish's back

eddy a circular water current, often created by an obstruction

exotic a foreign species, not native to a watershed, such as Zebra Mussel

fingerling a juvenile fish, generally 1 to 10 inches in length, in its first year of life

fork length the overall length of a fish from the mouth to the deepest part of the tail notch

fry a recently hatched young fish that has already absorbed its yolk sac

game fish a species regulated by laws for recreational fishing

gills organs used in aquatic respiration

gill cover large bone covering the gills, also called opercle or operculum

gill raker a comb-like projection from the gill arch

harvest fish that are caught and kept by sport or commercial anglers

ichthyologist a scientist who studies fish

invertebrates animals without backbones, such as insects, crayfish, leeches, and earthworms

lateral line a series of pored scales along the side of a fish that contains organs used to detect vibrations

mollusk an invertebrate with a smooth, soft body such as a clam and snail

native an indigenous or naturally occurring species

omnivore a fish or animal that eats plants and animal matter

opercle the bone covering the gills, also called the gill cover or operculum

otolith an L-shaped bone found in the inner ear of fish

panfish small freshwater game fish that can be fried whole in a pan, such as crappies, perch, and sunfish

pectoral fins paired fins on the side of the fish just behind the gills

pelvic fins paired fins below or behind the pectoral fins on the bottom (ventral portion) of the fish

pharyngeal teeth tooth-like structures found in the throat on the margins of gill bars

plankton floating or weakly swimming aquatic plants and animals, including larval fish, that drift with the current; often eaten by fish; individual organisms are called plankters

range the geographic region in which a species is found

ray, hard supporting part of the fin; resembles a spine but is jointed (can be raised and lowered) and is barbed; found in catfish, carp, and goldfish

ray, soft flexible structures supporting the fin membrane, sometimes branched

scales small, flat plates covering the outer skin of many fish

silt small, easily disturbed bottom particles smaller than sand but larger than clay

siltation the accumulation of soil particles

spawning the process of fish reproduction; involves females laying eggs and males fertilizing them to produce young fish

spines stiff, non-jointed structures found with soft rays in some fins

spiracle an opening on the posterior portion of the head above and behind the eye

standard length length of the fish from the mouth to the end of the vertebral column

stocking the purposeful, artificial introduction of a fish species into an area

swim bladder see air bladder

tapetum lucidum reflective layer of pigment in the eye of Walleyes

terminal mouth a type of mouth that faces forward

total length the length of the fish from the mouth to the tail compressed to its fullest length

tributary a stream that feeds into another stream, river, or lake

turbid cloudy; water clouded by suspended sediments or plant matter that limits visibility and the passage of light

vent the opening at the end of the digestive tract

ventral the underside of the fish; the opposite of dorsal

vertebrate an animal with a backbone

vomerine teeth found on the roof of the mouth

warmwater a non-salmonid species of fish that lives in water that routinely exceeds 70 degrees; also used to describe a lake or river according to average summer temperature

yolk the part of an egg containing food for the developing fish

zooplankton the animal component of plankton; tiny animals that float or swim weakly; common food of fry and small fish

PRIMARY REFERENCES

Bailey, R. M., and W. C. Latta, G. R. Smith. 2004
An Atlas of Michigan Fishes with Keys and Illustrations for Their Identification
University of Michigan Press

Becker, G. C. 1983
Fishes of Wisconsin
University of Wisconsin Press

Eddy, S., and J. C. Underhill. 1974
Northern Fishes
University of Minnesota Press

Hubbs, C. L., and K. F. Lagler. 1958
Fishes of the Great Lakes Region
University of Michigan Press

McClane, A. J. 1978
McClane's Field Guide to Freshwater Fishes of North America
Henry Holt and Company

Phillips, Gary L., and W. D. Schmid, J. C. Underhill. 1982
Fishes of the Minnesota Region
University of Minnesota Press

INDEX

173

ABOUT THE AUTHOR

Dave Bosanko was born in Kansas and studied engineering before following his love of nature to degrees in biology and chemistry from Emporia State University. He spent thirty years as staff biologist at two of the University of Minnesota's field stations. Though his training was in mammal physiology, Dave worked on a wide range of research projects ranging from fish, bird and mammal population studies to experiments with biodiversity and prairie restoration. An avid fisherman and naturalist, he has long enjoyed applying the fruits of his extensive field research to patterning fish location and behavior, and observing how these fascinating species interact with one another in the underwater web of life.